MORLOCKS IN THE BASEMENT

CAROLYN COLBURN

RUNNING
Wild
PRESS

CONTENTS

For my husband,
for his great temple of a heart

"Unnatural Basterds" appears in slightly different form in *What Sort of Fuckery is This?* (Devil's Party Press, 2019).

BED, BATH, AND ONE STEP
BEYOND

I n an effort to counter the flow of bad juju rising to the top
of our tank of late, my husband and I decided to take a
chance and get back in the game. Trip to Paris? new Beemer?
cosmetic surgery?

We got a kitten. From the local shelter. I could hear the
Stones in the background as we drove the little tuft of dryer lint
home.

Who tipped the scales at a staggering 3.2 pounds, was a
dead ringer for one of those miniature microfiber dust wands,
and wore a perpetual look of wholesale astonishment. Needless
to say the little afterthought weaseled her way into our brutal-
ized hearts within four seconds, and the rest is hearsay.

That was March. By August we'd almost killed her.

In July — blissfully unaware of the latest specter of pending
doom, and during a momentary psychotic break — I accidentally attended my high school reunion. Our forty-sixth. Which
number makes no sense, unless you're at the age where every

day — make that every minute — you find yourself still above-ground is a reason to celebrate. Let the party begin!

Looking back on it, having emerged from the primordial ooze of a three-week hangover, I was eventually able to discern God's plan. How playing four decades of CliffsNotes catch-up with similarly decaying classmates one hasn't seen since, well, one was still capable of actually seeing them, can shed light on one's own journey through this reality show we call *Life*.

Reality show my ass. The reality is, when it comes to things like reunions, everybody lies. About their ass. Where it's been, who it knows, how much money it makes, how it wouldn't know a plastic surgeon if one was living over the garage. And my ass is no different.

So there I am, swilling my seventeenth plastic cup of box wine, trying not to fall off my flip flops, holding forth on my remarkably fascinating and accomplished life to some shadowy humanoid leaning against the wall next to me, when I'm sucker-punched by a lightbulb moment: *I'm hallucinating! Flashbacking! Reporting in from some alternate universe!*

I'm making shit up. Time for another box, er, cup of wine.

Because the truth is, while I may have had my share of Kodak moments over the years, the larger portion of my life can be found drifting across the editing room floor like tumbleweed. As in, I've tumbled from scene to scene, decade to decade, era to era, endlessly searching for love, enlightenment, and that weed we used to smoke in the seventies.

The truth is, after the fifteen minutes are over and the curtain comes down and the lights go up and the rest of the staff heads for the nearest oxygen bar, it all comes down to this: housecleaning.

Housecleaning is what happens when you're dodging calls from the LA County Jail concerning "an incarcerated loved one."

When the road dead ends and the friends take a powder and the babies go *Poofff!!* and the drugs dry up and the center falls apart and the sex implodes and they fire your ass and the pets start dying and the housekeeper quits and the kid runs away and the lightning strikes twice and the house gets robbed and the car blows up and the gun goes off and your face keeps falling and the snow keeps piling and there's nothing left to do but shovel and vacuum and dust and drink.

This is after the gunfire and the chimney fire and the kitchen fire and the forest fire and before the garage burns down and god-knows-what-else, but who's counting?

During a lull in the action, we got the kitten.

In memory of the dogs — who of course were dead — we taught the kitten to fetch. Rather, my husband taught the kitten to fetch. You know those little cloth-covered rubbery hair bands, like little frisbees or boomerangs? *Poinnnggg!!* The kitten would tear-ass across the room, hellbent for rubber, like a little retriever. My husband even put it on YouTube, but I refuse to watch it, it makes me want to start Swiffering.

Then he went to Ireland. To golf. My husband no sooner left U.S. airspace than the kitten got sick. And sicker and sicker and sicker. That kitten was circling the drain, disappearing before my eyes, with me right beside her, dog paddling like a mofo. I mean, how much bad juju can a body take?

Remember this number: twelve. As in disciples, signs of the zodiac, months of the year, eggs in a carton, inches in a foot, roses in a vase, days of bad juju a body can take while a body's husband is off chasing his balls through the gorse.

As in the number of hair bands (*poinnnggg!!*) the veterinary surgeon found in the kitten's stomach when in a last-ditch effort to save even *one* of said kitten's lives, not to mention what's left of your own, you tear-ass down to The City for emergency exploratory surgery. On the kitten, not you.

By which time your husband has returned from the land of the leprechauns, pockets full of rye.

All's well that ends well, is what the well-wishers say. To which I say, how do you know when the fuck the end is?

Good news is, the little tuft of dryer lint survived. Miraculously the little ragmop recovered, and has since resumed her starring role in the reality show we call *Kitten*: tear-assing around, hellbent for rubber, hallucinating, making shit up, weaseling her way even further into our shattered souls.

I figure the little dustrag used up at least two of her nine lives in this little misadventure, but don't tell her. And speaking of ragmop-dustrag, while the kitten was convalescing in the temporary ICU of the mudroom, I cleaned this barn of a house to within an inch of *its* remaining life. Took me three weeks, with time off for debauched behavior.

I defy anyone to find anything remotely resembling a hair band in this drafty old dinosaur, I mean, I upended furniture that hasn't been moved since Hale-Bopp. I was like one of those mofos that lifts the car to save the ... kitten. With housemaid's knees to prove it.

Meanwhile, my husband continues to feel guilty, after all, the frisbee-hair bands were his idea. Except in the interest of full disclosure, I have to say the ponytail was my idea. For years I begged him to grow one, and he finally did, when he got tenure.

So it's a chicken/egg thing: what came first, my nagging ass, or my husband's hair bands? To which I say, let's just call the whole debacle a cautionary tale and have another box, er, cup of wine.

This was before my husband burned down the garage. But who's counting?

Good news is, the plastic surgeon who'd been living over the garage relocated to the mudroom the day before. Let the party begin!

CAROLYN COLBURN

LIFE SKILLS

The neighborhood I grew up in was crawling with children, it being the dawn of the Baby Boom, and the things tended to follow Yours Truly around like I was the Pied Piper.

No matter I was famous for knuckle-biting ghost stories that woke the little maniacs screaming in the night such that their mothers were forced to call my mother and demand a cease-and-desist. No matter my favorite backyard group games were Witch and Mental Man and Kidnap-and-Murder. No matter I regularly pretended to fall into a trance and wake up as a zombie or a cannibal. The little darlings kept coming back for more, hanging onto my every utterance, crowding around outside our back door like demented woodticks.

Fast forward a few eons. Seems I finally found a way to put this talent to good use. Meet the new preschool teacher, Yours Truly.

. . .

Believe me, Pre-K is not what it used to be. Forget naptime and Mister Potato Head. These days we have "curriculum" — Reading, Writing, Beginning Algebra, and something known as Life Skills. Things like making it to the bathroom on time and weapons concealment.

But I am pleased to report that old standby, Show and Tell, is alive and well.

On Wednesday one of the preschoolers gets up for Show and Tell.

"Actually I have a Tell," she says, and I say,

"Tell us," and she says,

"Actually my uncle died," and I say,

"Well I'm sorry," and she says,

"Actually he's in a coffin." And then she says,

"After two days he goes in the ground."

The room, which usually operates at a decibel level similar to the Jet Propulsion Laboratory, is instantly quiet. You can hear a pin drop. A feather. A Cheez-It. A coffin lid.

"Actually he's my great-uncle," she says. This girl likes to say "actually."

"My uncle's pretty great, too," says another girl, "and actually he didn't die." This girl likes to copy girl number one.

They're all sitting cross-legged on the big alphabet rug, looking at me. Waiting for me to say something. They want me to say something. They expect me to say something. Probably they're expecting me to say,

"Your uncle's in Heaven with Jesus, they're watching you *right this very minute.*"

Of course I can't say this. They listen to what I say. They believe what I say. They count on me. I've got to come up with something, fast. I stall for time.

"Ahhh ... will you have a funeral?" I ask girl number one.

"Not me," she says, "actually my uncle."

8

And there it is. Kids are so literal. That's the problem. You lie to them — *Santa Claus, the Easter Bunny, the Son of God* — they believe every word. Then when they're thirty-seven and finally figure things out, you're toast.

I remember exactly where I was when I figured it out about Santa Claus. Christmas Day, in the bedroom hallway, standing by the clothes chute (pronounced "cloe-shoot"). I'd spent the morning sashaying around the living room, back and forth in front of the Christmas tree, thanking Santa profusely for my new doll.

My sister finally decided she'd had enough.

"Actually," she commanded, "you should go into the kitchen and thank *Mother*."

I blinked. She looked at me like a know-it-all. Actually, she *was* a know-it all. I went into the kitchen.

"*Mom*-mee," I whined, rolling my eyes, "that know-it-all in there told me I should thank *you* for Betsy."

"Who's Betsy?" said Mommy, wiping her hands on her apron.

"*Bett*-see," I said indignantly, holding Betsy up in the air.

"Oh, *Betsy*," said Mommy, turning back to the breadboard. "Would you and Betsy like a little dough?"

Usually I'd jump at such an offer, but I was persistent.

"But why should I thank *you*?" I persisted. "What about *Santa?*"

"I'm busy right now, dear," said Mommy, the rolling pin closing in on warp nine. "Could you excuse me?"

By now I knew something was up. Locked in an intel-lectual-moral-spiritual dilemma, I returned to the living room.

"*We-ell?*" said my sister knowingly.

9

"Well *what*, you old poop," I said, and knocked over one of her cowgirl paper dolls.

Later that afternoon I cornered Mommy again in the bedroom hallway, where she was stuffing towels down the cloe-shoot. I tucked Betsy under my arm and tugged on Mommy's apron string.

"Mommy," I began, "what *about* Santa? What about him?" I could almost feel his presence hovering beside me in the bread-scented air.

Then came the moment I will never forget: Mommy shut the cloe-shoot, bent down, looked me in the eye.

"Well, dear," she said, "it's kind of a game we play."

The walls closed in, the floor swayed, the hallway darkened.

When my wits returned, I looked at Mommy hopefully. Hopefully I'd misunderstood. Hopefully I'd had a sudden conniption, a momentary blackout, and now it was over. But Mommy simply nodded her pretty head, and life as I knew it ended.

Mother (now I knew why my sister called her that) was a liar. My sister was omnipotent. I'd have to get an apartment and start drinking. *Santa Claus, the Easter Bunny, the Tooth Fairy, the Son of God* — it all disappeared in a yeasty puff as Betsy and I hung our heads and walked slowly away, into the yawning maw of a flat and soulless future.

I was thirty-seven.

Actually, I was seven. Which turned out to be a pivotal year in my life. It was also the year I became aware of boys.

My first crush was on Mighty Mouse. The one with muscles, not the skinny one. I pictured him rescuing me — from floods, speeding trains, evil-doers. After Mighty it was Ricky

Ricardo, followed by a boy in Reform School. I didn't know he was in Reform School until my sister pointed it out.

My sister was always pointing things out. *If you knot your kerchief on your chin, it means you're going steady. Horseback riding feels the same as You Know What. Too much Aqua Net causes brain damage. Don't wear the same blouse twice in one week, two weeks if at all possible.* After a dose of her advice, I'd look in the mirror and cringe. My hair still held the shape of the Spoolies, there was a gap between my front teeth wide enough to stick a fork in, I'd worn the same jumper for two years.

My sister had the wherewithal to have a crush on Elvis. Mighty Mouse didn't stand a chance in her book.

By the time I was in seventh grade, things had reached critical mass. So my sister, a junior in the same building, staged an intervention. She was popular, I was a liability. But by the time she was done with me, I was ready for my close up.

I'd learned how to rat my hair and walk out of the house backwards so my mother's ulcer wouldn't flare up. How to draw on eyebrows that didn't look like the heartbreak of psoriasis. How to smile with my lips closed until my gap grew in. She taught me to do the twist, to shorten my skirts by rolling up the waistband, which Gene Pitney songs were good for make-out practice.

When my sister left for college, it was like being fledged. One minute I'm twittering peacefully in the nest, the next thing I know, *BLAMMO!* Midair. I'd lost my mentor, my role model, my publicist. Although I'd gained a bedroom. At night, in my new room, I wrote her heart-wrenching letters about my boyfriend, about not making cheerleader, about the meaning of life. For emphasis I'd push on my eyeballs until teardrops splashed onto the page.

She wrote back saying she was voting for McCarthy and getting married.

Her marriage lasted about as long as Eugene's candidacy. By then I myself had migrated to The City, where I tucked up under her wing once again and tried to survive. The Big U. The War. Kent State. Nixon. Through it all, she pointed things out. *Wine is okay, just don't smoke pot. Pot is okay, just don't have sex. Sex is okay, just don't get pregnant.*

Following her lead, I accidentally got married. Likewise, divorced. Meanwhile, the seventies unfurled like a roll of shag carpet.

Then, the Crossroads.

To quote Steinbeck, *If you pick up the country and tilt it, all the loose stones will roll toward California.* California is what happened to my sister. One day she packed up her Toyota Celica with all her worldly possessions and drove Out West to check things out ... and it took. One look at that ocean, one whiff of eucalyptus, one movie-star sighting, she was hooked.

Through the years, she's tried to entice me to join her. And I have, many times. Cali is an awesome place to visit, dude. Only I wouldn't want to live there. Too many people. Too many vehicles filled with said people. Too many fault lines. Not that my chosen state is faultless ... incidentals like thirty-below-zero and firearms deer season come to mind.

But there's something about living in a place where the ground could open up at any moment and swallow you whole. Like sushi. At the very least shake you like a tossed salad. Where's Mighty Mouse when you need him? At least you can run away from a tornado. Sort of.

Maybe this is why my sister moves so often. Maybe she figures if she's been in a house or apartment for six or seven months without any tremors, her earthquake "window of luck" is running out, it's time to start over again somewhere new.

Actually, I'm planning to visit California again this summer. My sister tells me I'd better come in July, the house she just moved into is scheduled to be torn down in August. Who knows, maybe there'll be an earthquake, saving demolition costs. It'll be interesting staying in a place that's condemned. Sort of like growing up on the Mesabi Iron Range.

Where, thank my lucky stars, I had my sister to point things out. Which she's still doing.

At night, in my own room in my own house, I write her heart-wrenching emails about motherhood, mentally unstable bosses, waistline thickening due to aging. For emphasis I use emoticons instead of punctuation. She writes back saying *Nothing teaches perseverance like parenting. Going forward on one's Path is one's only job. Placentas from Russia work wonders.*

Then she says she's moving again and learning to levitate. Maybe if she masters the latter, the former will be moot. Then every time the earth moves, she can simply rise above it. Which is a life skill we could all use.

PLAYING HOUSE

When I was a young adult and had the energy for such things, I lived for a while without a phone, a television, or a car. I might've been making a statement about society, but it was also during a time when I would try pretty much anything to achieve an altered state, cultural deprivation included. I used the pay phone down on the corner, bought a bus pass, and cultivated a mild flirtation with an employee at the Uptown Theatre, who'd let me into film fests by way of the alley door and a quick bong hit.

First, I caved on the phone. I'd gone phoneless to discourage an ex-lover from calling fifty times a day. Eventually, having made sure Mr. Ex saw me with Bachelor Number Two — a guy three times his size who drove a perpetually-rebuilt Harley and hollered up at my window like Stanley Kowalski — I got an unpublished phone number and took my first baby steps back into civilization.

Next, I caved on the transportation. I bought my first and probably last new car, the Pony, a 1982 metallic blue Ford Mustang GT hatchback, which I rode for seventeen years until she died of natural causes. At which point I stripped her of all identifying marks, gathered up the loose change, old parking tickets, and empty beer cans from the floor of the back seat, wiped away my tears, and gave her to the American Lung Association for experimentation.

I probably could've gone on indefinitely without the television, but for the fact that Mr. Kowalski was currently in trade school studying to become, what else, a TV repairman. He regarded my tubeless state as nothing less than communist. One day, a short time before he drove off into the sunset in a mini mushroom-cloud of exhaust, he presented me with a used Motorola the size of a Sherman tank which he'd picked up for free at the People's Store over on Franklin. He shouldered the thing up to my third-floor apartment, parked it in the bedroom, hosed it down and resuscitated it, then spent the rest of our time together watching reruns of *The Rockford Files* and contemplating a possible road trip to Malibu to find out if the trailer court where Jim Rockford lived actually existed in reality. I spent the rest of our time together contemplating whether my boyfriend actually existed in reality.

This all happened down in The City, where I became a person. Or maybe just played one on TV.

I'm from the last generation not to be weaned on television.

My family didn't even own a TV until I was in grade school, when programs only appeared on one channel for a few hours in the afternoon, always through a gauzy veil of interference. From the outset my father declared jurisdiction over anything having to do with the television — On/Off, Vol., Vert. Hold, Hor. Hold — a precursor to today's male-dominated remote. Maybe he felt the thing needed male supervision, given that it might explode at any minute. Men, after all, were the ones who went to War. They had an innate sense of pending annihilation.

I knew about *Howdy Doody* and *Our Miss Brooks* and *My Friend Flicka*, and later Lucy and Ricky and Fred and Ethel and Rob and Laura. But I didn't grow up with them, I didn't confuse them with reality. I grew up with books, being more apt to believe there were little people the size of clothespins living under the floorboards, or that one day I'd answer the phone and it would be Trixie Belden needing my help.

Next to reading, playing house was my other all-time favorite childhood pastime. I was a house-playing junkie, certifiably doll-crazy. Storybook dolls, baby dolls, paper dolls — if it had a face, I played with it. As opposed to my present mantra, if it has a face, don't eat it. My dolls were more real to me than people. They had names, personalities, favorite wardrobe items, issues. They spoke to me. Literally. I was one of those kids who had imaginary friends, it's no stretch to envision me holding lengthy conversations with hunks of molded vinyl featuring rooted Saran hair and open-and-shut eyes.

An open-and-shut case of auto hallucination.

I hallucinated for the first time when I was three. It lasted five years.

That first out-of-body was likely brought on by a high fever, of which I seemed to have more than my share over the course of childhood. My sister, however, thinks I was having a vision, seeing beings "from the other side." My sister, after all, lives in California, where, I take it, you're never quite certain whether the person standing next to you actually exists in reality or not. (See above, re Jim Rockford's trailer court.)

At the time, back in those sepia-tinted days of the fifties, what I saw were two little adults, a male and a female, perfectly formed, only miniature. Exactly my size. They were absolutely real to me, indistinguishable from my sisters, the paperboy, or my best-friend-twice-removed. They even had names: Honey and Brother. They'd enter a room side-by-side, in step, like majorettes or Jehovah's Witnesses. They might've been married, possibly twins, possibly both. They'd walk right up and stand beside me and study my every move, and they never spoke. I was very comforted by them and considered them family. My family considered them a chore.

My parents would pat my head and prattle on about imagination and creativity while they plowed right through Brother's left flank, or ignored my heartfelt pleas on behalf of Honey, who stood quietly weeping at the curb as we drove off. My relatives weren't quite as magnanimous, their comments being more along the lines of *The kid's a buttonhead, must be the Finn side.* For anyone involved in my life, Honey and Brother were part of the package. *How come the kid's halfway down the clothes chute? What's the kid doing in the broom closet? Why's the kid talking to the dieffenbachia?*

Call them what you will — imaginary friends, visitors from the astral plane, symptoms of mental imbalance — Honey and Brother were a fact of life. Until the day I tried to conjure them.

It was a dark and stormy Saturday in late spring, second grade was nearing an end.

I was writing a play for Class Day, an off-off-off-Broadway hit featuring Harvey Ganarelli as the fat robber whose pants would fall down, Yours Truly as the beautiful gypsy princess who'd get to wear rouge and a fake braid for the performance. I'd been toiling over this masterpiece all morning. The rain was keeping me indoors, and my mother, anxious to get back to her preferred altered state — domestic euphoria brought on by a cocktail of coffee and Endust — was offering up ways to channel my excess creative energy.

Finally she suggested Honey and Brother. I hightailed it down to the rec room to set things in motion.

Except for this: they'd always just showed up, I'd never had to go looking for them. What was I supposed to do, pick up the phone? send a telegram? After a while I went upstairs, grabbed a broom, a mop, my father's favorite piano-playing sweater, and my fake braid, and brought it all back down to the basement. But where was I going with this? What in the Sam Hill was I doing?

I stood in the rec room my father had built — patterned linoleum floor, acoustical tile ceiling, knotty-pine walls — and it dawned on me: I was changing, emerging, becoming something else. Right there before my very eyes. Like a butterfly. I really felt this. Even at age eight. Even with a besweatered mop in hand. Even on the Iron Range.

After that time in the basement with the broom and the braid, I never saw Honey and Brother again. Although my sister thinks I could, if I really wanted to. It's her California showing.

One long-ago Christmas my father stayed up until dawn assembling child-sized cardboard kitchen and bedroom sets for me and my younger sister ("*Insert Tab A into Slot M-12 and have another bump*"), and my feelings about Santa took a biblical turn.

I homesteaded a corner of the downstairs rec room, arranged the new furniture in a state of feng shui delirium, and in an emotional homecoming ceremony, introduced my dolls to the new digs. My younger sister soon tired of such excessive domesticity and turned back to her new metal gas station unit. The takeover was complete.

I ruled the rec room for the next few years, as my doll family grew alongside my father's impatience. The original homestead continued to expand, and my father had to install a folding room divider to keep the dolls' house at bay so he could partition it off on poker nights. I'd crouch at the top of the basement stairs, bottle of grape Nesbitt's in hand, listening to the clink of ice cubes, the slap of cards, while puffs of cigar smoke circled up toward me like word balloons. Men's words, secret words, loud and foreign and unknowable.

And speaking of men, my other doll-crazy friends and I were aware of a major problem: there weren't any. They didn't exist in our world. There we were, living in a swoon of domestic bliss, surrounded by a passel of children, all of them girls, and not a husband in sight. But we resolved this handily: they'd all died in the War. Short and sweet, that's all she wrote. The War served simply to explain our manless state, allowing us to get on with the business of playing house.

My favorite doll-playing friend was Janet.

Janet lived in the house behind ours. She had a playhouse in the backyard, a ghost in the basement, and her face looked crooked in the bathroom mirror. Mostly we played little dolls, mostly my choice: kidnap and murder. I could get Janet to do just about anything.

Once I got her to ask me to sleep over. We had Chef-Boy-Ar-Dee for supper, prowled around looking for the ghost, watched *Twilight Zone*, played phone tricks ("Good evening, madam, is your refrigerator running? You better catch it!"). When her mother told us lights out, sweet dreams, and closed the bedroom door, I fell apart and had to go home. I might've been bossy, but I was also a spastic homesick crybaby.

Janet's mother was from Florida and had dyed black hair and red toenails. She was overweight but knew how to wear it. She wore pedal pushers and beachwalkers and hung a sign in her kitchen: "Why is there always so much of the month left at the end of the money?" Our mothers would get together for coffee at one another's dinette tables, and afterwards Janet and I would pretend to smoke their lipsticked cigarette butts and promise to stay best friends.

Our mothers were best friends until Janet's mother had an affair with the butcher on First Avenue. The store where the butcher worked had wooden floors, his apron was always bloody. Janet's father worked in the mines, his overalls were always muddy. On washdays Janet's father's overalls hung on the clothesline like so many bodies. He never said much, but he must have said something, because Janet's mother lost fifty pounds and moved back to Florida. She left her husband, her kids, and the butcher behind, but took along Mr. Robison, the father of another doll-playing friend of ours. Eventually they got married, and she became Mrs. Robison.

Once, years later, my mother ran into Janet's mother in a department store a couple of towns over. *The Graduate* had just been released, and my mother couldn't help herself. *"Here's to you, Mrs. Robison!"* she blurted, raising an invisible cocktail. She giggled about her chutzpah for years afterward.

Meanwhile, Janet's father got remarried and started talking more. The new wife was skinny and wore glasses and didn't hang signs in her kitchen. Occasionally they played pinochle and drank highballs with my parents. By this time Janet and I were in high school, our friendship light-years behind us. We moved in different solar systems and acknowledged one another like spaceships passing in the night whenever our orbits intersected.

I was as bossy as ever, but when my lying-son-of-a-lying-son-of-a-bitch boyfriend broke my heart, I began nonstop spastic crying. After a few weeks of this, my mother sent me into the backyard, where I sat hunched atop the picnic table, staring through my veil of tears at Janet's house, willing her to notice me. After a while the back door opened, and Janet walked over. Her face wasn't crooked anymore. I wanted to get her to do something — play dolls, make pizza, change my life — but I'd gotten her to come over, which was somehow enough.

After high school Janet moved to Florida and disappeared. Florida and California were similar that way, a couple of black holes sucking up all who came within a hair's breadth of their forcefields. Meanwhile, I packed up my Trixie Beldens, gave away my dolls and my cardboard Dream House, bid farewell to the place where I grew up, and headed down to The City.

A move which, in spite of my manless state, or perhaps because of it, allowed me to get on with the business of becoming a person.

Short of moving to California, I *have* tried to conjure Honey and Brother again over the years, in a number of ways — roller skating, midway rides, the woods, a Gibson 335 — but mostly I've tried through various controlled substances.

Acid, for instance, which I took a number of times, the first something called Green Pyramid. Curious how it always had those two names, and that was me, curiouser and curiouser, like Alice. I sat in a bathroom astride a clawfoot tub and gave my undivided curiosity to the wallpaper, where the secret of life was being revealed. My boyfriend *du jour* got pissed off and dumped me because I'd managed to hallucinate the very first time — sort of like orgasm — whereas he'd been trying for seven-and-a-half years and hadn't yet achieved it. Hallucination, that is. So he stomped down the stairs and out the door and rode his Dodge Dart back to Wisconsin. A few days later I left the bathroom.

Then there was the shroom phase, when I was revealed in the cattails on the banks of Lake Harriet, inspiring me to roller skate to Canada and back. Followed by the white cross phase, shroom phase II, the Hollywood diet phase, the Hollywood diet redux, and so on.

These days I'm in the endorphin phase. I've exchanged my Oberhamers with City Roller Wheels for Saucony 3D Grid Hurricanes. I can be revealed in the clouds at the finish of a 10k, or during a midnight trek to the outhouse at the cabin on a full-moon midnight in winter. I'm now a cheap date when it comes to altered perception, just getting out of bed in the morning can be a trip.

And all in pursuit of some elusive longing for revelation, for that state of grace which once permeated my childhood, and which, with or without the fake braid, I seem to have lost.

Maybe on my deathbed I'll get back there. To the garden. I'll be laid out on some gurney in some ICU, or sprawled across some sidewalk or street, or splayed out across the floor of the Canadian Shield on a full-moon midnight in winter, and two familiar figures, exactly my size, will sidle up and start studying my every move. Maybe the metaphorical wallpaper will start to move all around us, and the secret of life will finally be revealed.

Or maybe it will turn out it's all been a dream — like season seven of *Dallas* — and everybody will wake up in California. Maybe Florida.

For most of my adult life, when I can't sleep, I take out this fantasy: I'm in a mansion, hiding behind a curtain — or under a table or in a closet — peering out at a crowd. People dressed to the nines, drinking champagne, speaking politely. The thrill is that no one knows I'm there. All-knowing, the watcher. Like God.

My daughter must feel something similar, as her small hand tucks a knit cap into the umbrella barrel. Does she look up through her bangs, between the red and blue partitions, at her classmates eating their Roll Ups? I wish I could be there, crouched behind the patrol flags, a fly on the wall.

My daughter is stealing things at school. Well, hiding things. Other kids' stuff, in the cloakroom, when they're having snack time. At the end of the day, when the other kids search for missing mittens and boots, my daughter miraculously finds them. The teacher thinks this is her way of being the hero.

When my daughter was born, her birth mother called. My niece. It's a girl, five pounds, her hair is brown, she said. I was in another state, cleaning the bathroom, the phone cradled against *my ear like a shell. When she hung up, I kept the phone at my ear, listening for the sea. When she called back, four years later, I said,* Yes, I'll take her, send her to me.

As we walk through the late afternoon sun with the dog, my daughter walks a few yards ahead. Pretend you're lost, that you don't know me, that you follow me home, *she says. At our front door she turns, looks surprised to see me. She says,* This is my house, it's humongous, do you want to live here with me?

After the first ectopic, my husband and I moved to the woods. For a while? forever? Who could know. We brushed trail, photographed deer, walked by the river, learned birds. Day by day the trees absorbed our great sorrow. A year passed, then another, then five more. One evening I found myself deep in the trees, leaning against a spruce trunk, watching a bear in the clearing. Her great paw moved carefully through the thistle, her pink tongue stretched toward the raspberries. The thrill was that she didn't know I was there. And that I did.

My daughter is asking what's real. She ticks off her list — Easter Bunny? Tooth Fairy? Mother Nature? *She saves the big one for last.* Santa Claus?, *she says, her brown eyes watching, and I'm thinking,* God. She doesn't even ask about God. But then, why should she? *We've never offered her God. Only a bicycle, a bird feeder, a yellow bedroom, a family. A forever family, is how we say it.*

And in a few years, if she suddenly turns to me and asks, I wonder if I'll be ready. I wonder if I'll be able to say, Yes, that's one of them. Forever is real.

KEEPING HOUSE

My daughter ran away last week. But don't look for her on a milk carton.

I figured she ran away to the back seat of the Jeep, one of her usual getaway places. Another is the third-floor bathroom storage cupboard. Still another is behind the old wingback in the dining room, though the fit is getting a bit tight.

Let's say we needed our space. I sat on the third-floor landing, watching the Jeep down on the driveway through the dormer window. It was late afternoon. I imagined I could see her there, in the back seat, and then the sun would slant just so through the birch leaves, and she'd disappear. I kept vigil for over an hour, but I was keeping vigil on a shadow. Turns out she'd run away to the next-door neighbor's.

The next-door neighbor is a police officer. The first time I saw this neighbor in her work get-up, it was dusk of a summer evening. We'd recently moved into our new/old house in town. I was walking through the kitchen, minding my own business, when I glanced into the backyard and froze. A cop was standing out on the deck.

The stash!? where's the stash!? gotta flush the stash!?
Your basic seventies flashback.

So it's a good news/bad news thing. Your daughter decides to run away. She runs away to a cop's house.

When I was a kid, I never ran away. Although once my mother tried to get me to leave. She packed a suitcase, put it out on the front porch, put me out next to it, and went back inside and locked the door. I was ten, my daughter's age now. I remember sitting on the porch on the suitcase, planning my future. *Gotta make it to the dumps ... carry the suitcase ... make camp ... build a fire ... did Mom pack matches? ... did she pack my mimi? ... did she pack Trixie Belden? ... how do you build a fire? ... what if Haven Court boys show up? ... what if they have rubber guns??!!*

Raise your hand if you've ever been shot with a rubber gun. On your bare legs. On the Mesabi Iron Range. In the fifties.

Now that I'm a parent, I understand how one can get pushed to the point of sending one's child packing. Better yet, how about sending oneself packing. I'm picturing a beach, a line of umbrella drinks, a leaning tower of *People*.

Actually I did run away, twice. Once when I was twenty-five, again when I was thirty. Both times to escape Mister Wrong. When Mister Wrong One realized I'd taken a powder, he wanted to throw me in front of a bus. When Mister Wrong Two had a similar realization five years later, he wanted to throw a party.

My mother eventually summoned me back inside from the porch — back into the family, her heart, her kitchen. Where I chose creamed-peas-on-toast for my special homecoming dinner, my all-time favorite comfort food. Your basic WWII flashback.

Creamed Peas on Toast / Shit on a Shingle

1 can green peas
2 tbs Smart Balance
3 tbs flour
½ cup almond milk

In small pot on stove slowly melt butter, add flour, add milk, add peas.
Dump the whole mess on a piece of toast.

To borrow from Nixon, "I am not a cook." But I have learned a few kid pleasers, pea soup being one. My daughter's all-time favorite comfort food is pea soup. Which I made again last week, and froze a good portion of, to be thawed out on an as-needed basis.

Pea Soup

1 cup olive oil
2 lg yellow onions
18-20 cloves garlic
6 lg celery stalks
2 pkgs vegan ham slices
1 lb split peas
6 lg carrots
4 largish potatoes
(salt, pepper, cayenne, parsley, dill, bay leaves, celery seed, basil, Spike!, splash balsamic)

Saute (heat slowly w/o starting fire) the first four ingredients (chopped, diced, minced, whatever) in big ass pot on stove. Add wine (to you, not the pot). When celery is mooshy, add 8-3/4 cups water + peas + spices (amounts vary). Add wine (a couple more glasses to you, a dash to

the pot). When peas begin to moosh up, add carrots +
potatoes + a bunch more water. Celebrate with wine,
you're pretty much done, except for the simmering
part. Simmer partly covered for a while, then uncov-
ered at the end for a while. Drink wine. (*Prep to finish,
8-10 hours, give or take)

When my cell phone rings in public, I panic. My cell plays
"The Drinking Song" from *La Traviata*. Say I'm at Target, my
phone rings. I'm momentarily transported before panic sets in.
Sometimes I'll let it keep ringing, a sort of operatic Muzak
while I decide what grade toilet paper to buy.

A while back I picked up a white horse in the 75% OFF!
aisle. It looked vaguely Chinese and spoke to me. I couldn't
believe it hadn't been snatched up for the original $39.95. I
took it out of the bag and set it on the front passenger seat,
facing forward, while I drove home. It's become an object of joy
to me. I *neigh!* to it and stroke it like a buddha when we pass in
the hallway. That is, I pass, it stands unmoving on its pedestal.

My daughter rolls her eyes and turns up her MP3 player
whenever she sees me around my horse. She's my go-to when it
comes to web-surfing, DVD-ing, CD-ing, anything vaguely
electronic. If I notice a missed call on my cell, I hand it over to
her with shaking hand and she retrieves the message. Sometimes she changes my ringtone, and I'm startled out of my
reverie at Menards by the Laurel and Hardy theme song.

No one ever calls me on my cell except my husband. Sometimes he calls from the third floor, wondering if the coffee is
ready yet. Or the wine. A couple of years ago you could make
book on my never getting a car phone, er, cell phone. It feels
like I've only recently gotten the hang of microwaving. And I
consider the existence of my personal email account a minor

miracle, given that I still believe my computer could blow up at any minute. I mean, literally blow up.

Before I took my horse home, I checked it out thoroughly. The Trojan factor. I didn't want any last minute digital surprises, like a hidden clock under its tail, or a calculator or fax machine. But it's all horse. Although I've resisted naming it. I'm good at certain name categories — dogs, cats, dolls, kids, dickhead redneck mouthbreathers — but I feel somewhat equestrian-challenged. Secretariat is the best I can come up with.

Maybe I'm going through a latent "adolescent-girl-obsessed-with-horses" phase. As opposed to "adolescent-girl-obsessed-with-houses," which *I* used to be, filling notebook after notebook with detailed variations on My Dream House, its central feature an enormous slide spiraling down from the fourth floor to the swimming pool in the basement. I could hardly wait for the "House of the Week" supplement in the Sunday newspaper and would sprawl out on the wall-to-wall carpeting and study it for hours, while my sister, from the comfort of the three-piece sectional couch, studied her well-thumbed edition of *American Horse* and twirled her long brown ponytail.

Maybe My New Improved Dream House should feature an open floor plan surrounding a central stable, like the Norwegians. I could start with faux hay and horses on pedestals and see how it went.

I asked my daughter if she'd be able to change my cell phone's ringtone to "The William Tell Overture," if need be. She stared at me a nanosecond longer than usual before her eyes rolled up into their sockets. And no, she wasn't having a seizure, it's that involuntary adolescent twitch she's been battling for some time now. I might have to figure the ringtone thing out for myself.

* * *

CAROLYN COLBURN

Among a plethora of things — thunderstorms, red states, department store clerks, anyone who wears orange camo, anyone who says irregardless, anyone who says plethora — I'm afraid of the housekeeper. Deep in my heart I know I should be ashamed I have a housekeeper. Sometimes it concerns me that my daughter is growing up not knowing her way around a vacuum. She can out-tech me, out-cook me, out-run me, out-smart me until the cows come home, but she thinks it's okay to spray Shout! on the TV screen.

The housekeeper is a cleaning machine, from the Old School. The one my mother attended, where you learned to Do It Right. Down to lemon-juicing the doorknobs and tooth-pasting the silver service. My mother *was* a housekeeper — she had a house, and she kept it. Spotless. Shipshape. Spick-and-span. Although every spring, she hired The Girl.

She'd hire the girl for a week, and together they'd turn our modest three-bedroom rambler inside out on a vision quest to ferret out every last smidgeon of dust and dirt from every last cranny. The girl was a Mennonite and wore a small silver cross over a long shapeless dress, and a stiff little netted pillbox affair, which resembled meringue, at the back of her head. Her hair was braided tightly inside the meringue, further enhancing the pastry effect, and she wore no makeup.

The presence of this girl in our midst for a week every spring gave new meaning to the old adage regarding cleanliness and godliness. I remember coming home from school and finding the two of them — the girl and my mother — taking a break at the gray Formica dinette table, drinking coffee out of bone china cups from the collection displayed in a shadow box hanging on the wall behind them. They weren't praying, they were laughing. Make that giggling. They made an odd pair, this Plain Girl, with her shapeless clothes and secret braid, and my modern American mother, with her matching lips and nails and Jackie Kennedy bouffant.

But they had one thing in common: they could clean the fuck out of a house.

My housekeeper isn't a Mennonite, but I wish she were. In place of a long gray dress and a net pillbox, my housekeeper sports jeans and a frown. I'm afraid of my housekeeper, not because she's Christian (in my limited observation they make better house cleaners), but because she's the F word: Fundamentalist Christian. I discovered this after the fact, after she'd been cleaning my house for a few months. By that time I was addicted to the way the porcelain squeaked and the floors shone like a hockey rink when she got done with them, and it was too late.

There's something about FCs, about the way they look at you. Or rather, don't.

The housekeeper turns books and magazines face down if she considers their covers offensive. This includes anything with a hint of a possibility of cleavage. Which means I have to go around the house after she's left and re-right all the reading material, with the exception of *National Geographic Kids* and *L.L.Bean Holiday Collection*. I've come home unexpectedly to find the radio blaring some FC station loud enough to be heard up on the third floor, where she's cleaning the fuck out of the shower stall and stacking back issues of *Vanity Fair* upside down behind the toilet, all the while, presumably, praying, likely for me. Believe me, this woman can multitask.

Once I made the mistake of asking her a harmless bit of parenting advice (nothing along the lines of what to do if your child wants a head tattoo), and I got the standard FC all-purpose "Let go and let God," delivered with a flourish of dustrag and an all-knowing nod. It made me want to let go, all over the rug. I started looking around for a Bible to turn over, irregardless of the fact that there wasn't a Bible in sight, only a plethora of cleavage mags, this being my house and all.

Maybe I'm too much the pagan to raise my cleaning standards to a higher power, er, level. Not that I don't occasionally entertain a hint of a possibility of the miraculous. For instance, I consider cooking to be a miracle, pea soup in particular. The housekeeper would probably find this blasphemous. She might even ask *me* to turn over. I'm sure the mere sight of me might be offensive to any number of FCs, not to mention red staters, department store clerks, dickwads in orange camo. I should probably include my mother in that list, but let's not go *there*. To be fair, my mother came of age in a different era, a time when you ironed the bed linens and read Heloise religiously. I'm still coming of age. Or likely just aging.

Not to put too fine a point on it, I have done my share of housecleaning over the years, to say nothing of cleaning house. I'm just in a different place these days. A very clean place, it would seem. At least on the surfaces.

The last time she showed up to whip my cave into shape, the housekeeper asked if this time of year is difficult for me. This was just after Thanksgiving, the aroma of tofurky still lingered. I assumed she was referring to my status as a newly mother-less/fatherless child, and so I answered, *Yes, I sorely miss them, thank you for asking*.

My bad.

Actually she was referring to my faithless pagan state, during this most sacred time.

And speaking of faux poultry.

The look of concern on her face belied the fact that she also felt compelled to relate the story of how, a few years back, she and her husband single-handedly slaughtered 150 chickens in a shed on their property, which resulted in a bit of a bloodbath, which attracted a skunk, which sprayed the dog, whose eventual fate at their hands I prefer not to revisit.

And people wonder why I'm afraid of this creature.

I'd just come up from the basement sauna, swaddled in a towel, and was leaning against the wall to keep from collapsing in a swoon, when I was surprised to find the housekeeper standing in the kitchen, mop in hand. She'd arrived early. Which is when she commented on it being a difficult time of year for such as myself. Compromised though I was, in my humble loincloth, I held it together. I said many people regard Thanksgiving as a secular holiday, and as for that other upcoming holiday, I and mine would be celebrating the Winter Solstice, *thankyouverymuch*, back by popular demand after centuries of neglect, and which predates Christmas by epochs, if not eons.

And with that, I exited, carefully, up the stairs.

If I wasn't so lily-livered I'd fire her ass and hire Merry Maids, although my liver is anything but lilied. Let's just say I'm chicken. Among a plethora of things — change hairdressers, go to the dentist, go to the mall, cancel Satellite, watch Al Gore's movie — I'm chicken to test my liver enzymes. And as for Mr. Gore — preaching to the choir, and all that — I live in the Far North of North, where it's already mid-December and there's not even a hint of a possibility of snow. This is the same neck of the woods where my father had to call his office to send over a front-end loader to dig us out of the house one memorable January morning back in childhood.

Now here I sit, sipping shade-grown Columbian in my cozy belfry, looking out my window, and it's raining! Cats and dogs! Chickens! Hypocrites!

But according to the housekeeper, there's no such thing as global warming, or evolution, or the theory of relativity, take your pick. There's only some poor little schmuck in a loincloth in a manger and some sheep and cows and goats and stoner shepherds. The FCs talk about intelligent design, a sort of *"Pay No Attention to the Man Behind the Curtain!"* explanation, like Santa could be running the show. Only he better watch out, the North Pole is fast disappearing.

And it *is* difficult for me this time of year. Just when I think my season in hell is over for another ten months, *i.e.,* firearms deer season, all those bright plastic figures start popping up on my neighbors' lawns like some kind of grotesque fungus, the newest craze being an enormous blow-up Santa with Rudolph prancing around inside him, where his stomach oughtta be. Or his liver.

But this is the way we do it here in America, this is our intelligent design. *New at Menards!* Jesus might have gone in search of that missing lamb, but rest assured it will end up inside a couple million enormous blow-up stomachs, along with a couple of stray chickens and the odd deer shank.

Merry Christmas! Merry Maids! Mary Had A Little Lamb ... with mint sauce!

FOOD CHAIN

A sister of one of the preschoolers named her new Barbie after me. I told my daughter, thinking this would impress her.

"Mom, she's two," said my daughter.

So? Today she's two, tomorrow she's accepting a Pulitzer and thanking her sister's preschool teacher. Or maybe her Barbie, whom she named after me.

I was ten when Barbie was born. She appeared suddenly, miraculously, from the mind of God. Like Jesus. My younger sister and I each had our own Barbie — the ponytail blonde, the bouffant brunette — and would painstakingly dress them in the latest fashion, then switch heads when we wanted to change outfits.

I can think of a few women I'd like to switch heads with. So can my husband.

These days the preschoolers don't switch heads, they just buy ten new Barbies. It's all too much, too overwhelming. So in the interest of the teacher's mental health, and in an effort to bring these demented woodticks into the 21st century, I've found it necessary to declare Show and Tell a Barbie-free zone.

Last week one of the boys brought a pair of headphones for Show and Tell. At least I thought they were headphones. He's a shy kid, barely audible, who tends to cry when he gets dropped off in the morning. As soon as his parent-of-the-moment leaves the classroom, I bend down and look into his eyes and tell him he knows his mother / father / grandmother / aunt is coming back, crying is inappropriate, get over to the goddamn art table *NOW!*

(*Not! Just kidding!*)

So this kid, let's call him Randall, gets up for Show and Tell, and he's got this big ass pair of headphones like from the seventies, when we all looked like astronauts connected by lifelines to our stereo systems across the room. I ask him what he listens to with these headphones, and he looks at me like I'm an astronaut. He answers so softly I have to ask him to repeat.

"Nothing," he whispers.

"You listen to *nothing?*" I say.

He nods. I check the clock. I can actually hear it ticking. Which means the room has quieted down from the usual Metrodome roar. Have I mentioned Randall is one of only two boys in the class? This means the remainder are girls. Aren't we always? And the remainder always quiets down to hear what the quotient has to say. Or something like that.

So because Randall is Randall, and I'm dreamily enjoying a momentary lull in the decibel level, it takes some time to get the true story of the headphones. Which are indeed not head-phones, as per my conjecture. Nor are they earmuffs, as per Gina's. They are in fact ear protectors, used to stop noise. What sort of noise?

"Shooting," whispers Randall.

"Shooting?" I whisper, lowering my voice to match his. I can taste the blood on my tongue from biting it.

"My dad takes me shooting," whispers Randall.

Have I mentioned that most of Randall's clothing is camo? Earlier this year he brought a set of antlers to school for Show and Tell. Very small antlers. I made him leave them in his cubby, and when he wasn't looking, I covered them gently with his camo mittens and had a moment of silence.

"Your dad's a fucking asshole," I whisper.

(*Kidding!*)

Randall is so soft-spoken, the "shooting" bit doesn't appear to register with the other kids. They just want to take turns trying on the "earmuffs," no doubt to experience the thrill of not hearing their teacher's voice for a few nanoseconds.

Later, when I'm rounding everyone up for snack time, I can't find Randall. He's not answering. Eventually I find him in the bathroom, standing on the stepstool at the sink, holding his hands under the faucet and humming softly while water runs between his fingers like a tiny waterfall. He's wearing the earmuffs. When I touch his shoulder, he jumps. I have to catch him to keep him from falling off the stool.

Last Tuesday the preschoolers celebrated the ever-popular Earth Day. A questionable celebration at best, as if we can stop this climactic apocalypse in its traces. Like visiting your terminally-ill mother in the ICU and handing her a balloon, which you are confident will bring her back from the brink.

Still, in honor of this dubious occasion, a couple of scientists from the EPA showed up to talk to the preschoolers about life at the microscopic level, specifically at the bottom of The Big Lake. They came with their microscopes and their cool underwater videos and their petri dishes of diverse interesting aquatica, and aside from my ongoing efforts at rescuing errant bloodworms and water fleas from certain death by paper towel, it was a success.

At the closing "lecture," which he repeated four times to four different classes, Scientist Mr. Dan drew a picture on the dry-erase board. First he drew waves. Next, a circle of algae beneath the waves. Beside the algae he drew a creature he called Mr. Plankton, and beside Mr. Plankton, a fish with a big open mouth. Scientist Mr. Dan talked about how Mr. Plankton needed algae for food, and how Mr. Fish needed Mr. Plankton for food, and then he asked the class what would happen to Mr. Fish if Mr. Plankton were gone, whereupon the preschoolers shouted joyously, *"He would starve!"*

(*FYI, preschoolers love to shout joyously, together, on cue.*)

Finally, Scientist Mr. Dan drew a boat atop the waves, and a man in the boat.

(*Actually it was a stick figure, but seeing as the male pronoun was the default setting for everything else in Scientist Mr. Dan's day-long blather, I made an assumption, which proved correct. Where's Barbie when you need her?*)

The man in the boat was holding a fishing pole, and the line reached down beneath the waves and ended with a big hook suspended in the water beside Mr. Fish. At this point Scientist Mr. Dan turned to the class and asked what the man in the boat was doing, whereupon the preschoolers shouted, *"He's catching the fish!"*

(*The only problem being that Mr. Man wouldn't die if he didn't have Mr. Fish to eat, he could simply choose to eat something else, for instance, Ms. Broccoli-Tofu-Casserole-with-a-Nice-Chardonnay, but I kept these thoughts to myself.*)

The first three classes went swimmingly, each ending with the joyous chorus, *"He's catching the fish!"*

Then it was our turn, the last class, the one I teach. We got through the videos and the microscopes and the petri dishes and nary a bloodworm nor a water flea perished. At last, Scientist Mr. Dan gathered us together for his final lecture. When he finished his drawing of the algae and the plankton and the fish and the hook, he turned and asked his final important question. And Charmaine knew the answer. Immediately. Before any of the rest of us could open our mouths, Charmaine told us exactly what the man in the boat was doing:

"*He's saving the fish!*"

Scientist Mr. Dan was at a loss. For words, among other things.

"Way to goddamn go, Char*maine!*" I shouted joyously. (*Not!*)

Afterward, at snack time, I couldn't decide what to give the newly-anointed Junior Scientists. Animal crackers? goldfish? After such a harrowing day, I just couldn't do it, and I silently declared a lifeform-free zone.

I looked down at the earnest little darlings, crowded around me, hanging onto my every utterance, and I gave them the only snack my inner voices could agree on: *sugar!* The ultimate kid drug. In the form of M&Ms, many many many M&Ms, which we lined up and sorted and counted and devoured, and then, joyously shouting all the M words we could think of, we galloped over to the big blue alphabet rug and had ourselves a fucking dance party.

Last night when I was putting my daughter to bed, we came up with three rules to live by:

1. Brush your teeth
2. Bus your dishes
3. Don't get stabbed

My daughter worries that I'm going to die. Not necessarily tomorrow, but in a general sense. She usually brings up the Death Thing when she's sick, or anxious about something else — an upcoming gymnastics meet, a social studies test, guilt over a 48-hour filibuster of nonstop backtalk. Such excess exhausts even her, the poor dear. In this instance, she was concerned about something her boyfriend said.

Okay, it's more like he's a friendboy. I mean, these kids have known each other since kindergarten, it's so cute. Just this summer they kicked it up a notch and decided to call themselves BF-and-GF. She confided all this to me one night back in July when she had strep throat and was worried I was going to die.

"It's so nice to have a friend-that's-a-boy," I said, knocking back a shot of her prescription cough medication when her head was turned.

"M-*om*," she croaked from the depths of her sickbed, "he's my *boy*friend, promise me you're not going to die."

"Keep this up and I won't be buying any unripe bananas," I muttered under my breath, but she was coughing too loudly to hear, the poor thing.

This kid's an okay kid, I guess, it's hard to tell. He's a man of few words. My husband and I can hardly get him to complete a sentence, the 1,000-watt bulb and tape recorder notwithstanding. For my money, the main points in his favor are:

1. Okay grades
2. Longish hair
3. Crying in kindergarten whenever his mother left

My daughter tells me he'll occasionally shed a tear or two around her. Not as many as he's going to shed if I ever ... but I'm getting ahead of myself. Come on, it's just too cute, kids these days.

My first kiss happened when I was fourteen, up against the dumpster behind Cobb Cook Grocery. It was the darkest corner He could find, the alley light being conveniently broken. He'd been conveniently eyeing the spot for weeks. I'm talking He, as in my first love. Who's since gone on to wearing half-buttoned shirts with multiple gold necklaces in some non-coastal Western state. Or so I tell myself.

But back in 1964, he was the real thing. As in, *Why do the backs of my knees feel funny?* There was his cowlick, his crooked tooth, the way he held a baseball bat. There was that first dumpster dive, followed by an escalating series of others, until we'd morphed from the back alley to the backseat of a Pontiac LeMans out by the ore dumps north of town.

My point being, I know how these things go. I remember, I'm talking species memory here. I look at my daughter after she's been hanging out with this long-haired crybaby, and I ask her if her knees feel funny. This is the same daughter who came home from school one day in second grade and called a family meeting, saying she had an announcement to make. My husband and I sat on the edge of the couch hyperventilating while she cleared her throat.

"Mom, Dad, it's official," she said, and you could almost hear the drum roll. "I'm a tomboy."

I wanted to break out the champagne, having feared something more along the lines of "*Am I old enough to get permanent eyeliner tattoos?*" My husband and I let out a collective breath and fairly wept with joy and relief. Joy, because it wasn't the eyeliner thing. Relief, because maybe just maybe we'd somehow manage to circumvent all that BF-and-GF crap and Pass Go and Collect $200 and have this kid packed off to some college somewhere before her hormones staged a major coup and we'd have to move to the garage.

And for the past four-and-a-half-years our daughter has

been in major tomboy mode. Her closet and dresser drawers are overrun with athletic wear, her bathroom shelf is a Maybelline-free zone, she races (and cartwheels and backhands and round-offs) her way through life in boys' Nikes. She fake-barfs whenever she sees pink, considers Britney Spears to be one notch below plant life, and has officially given me all of her dolls.

But for the past week, ever since her first day of middle school, there's been a change in the weather. Now we've got the nail polish thing (it's black, but still), the eye makeup thing (barely noticeable for school, all-out zombie in the privacy of her own mausoleum), the outfit thing (we used to do clothes, now we do fashion). Just before school started she called in her Good Grades All Year Award from last year and had the hairdresser dye her hair two-shades-shy-of-Elvira. While I wouldn't call the new look goth, exactly, we're tilting in that direction. But who am I to talk, you need a flashlight to distinguish between all the black in my closet.

I wonder if this ... climate adjustment ... has something to do with the BF? Or maybe it's all those skaggy seventh-and-eighth-grade girls parading through the halls at the new school? Or maybe it's ... Mother Nature knock-knock-knocking at her door??

Sometimes at night I'll still stand in the hallway outside her bedroom door just listening to her sleep. It's one of those things parents do, basking in the holy silence of a child's unconsciousness. When she was younger I used to step into the room to adjust a blanket, return a stray foot to the fold, stroke a warm brow. Not anymore. This summer she hung a half dozen gymnastics medals on the doorknob, effectively creating a tri-county alarm system. To keep out knife-wielding maniacs. Mother Nature. Mother.

At least she still worries about my mortality. She mentioned it again last weekend when she had that twenty-four-hour bug that's been going around. It's those little things a parent clings to.

My daughter and I were driving home from a gymnastics meet last weekend. Several days after the eclipse, the horizon washed red with sunset, stars sparking to life all around.

"Mommy," she said, blinking sleepily in the dashboard light, "what's a boner?"

Thank God for cruise control.

When my vision cleared, I mentally counted three beats. I read that somewhere.

"Have you been watching *Desperate Housewives* again?" I asked.

My daughter is on a *Desperate Housewives* kick. She's made it to Season Four. When I questioned her about it, she told me it's her *Sopranos*. I had a fleeting image of lying in the recliner in the flickering TV light, watching Tony and Christopher subdivide Richie, while my daughter knocked forlornly on the bedroom door like the Little Match Girl.

"*No*," she said. "I mean *yes*," she said. "I mean *why*?" she said.

"Well, honey, it's just that, I don't know, sweetie, I was just wondering where, you know, you might've *heard* that word?" I sounded like a Chatty Cathy doll. Someone should sever my string.

"Math," she said.

"Math?" I said.

A Peterbilt rocketed past in the left lane. Where's the State Patrol when you need them? Probably home watching the *Sopranos*.

"The math assistant," she said. "Madison says he rubs against her in fractions. He's got a boner, she says."

I'm having multiple reactions. First, the obvious. Anyone

who would name their kid Madison, well, I rest my case. Second, if it's true, someone should string this fractionalized dweeb up by his gonads. Where's Tony Soprano when you need him? Third, how do I proceed with this PowerPoint presentation?

I distinctly remember asking my own mother where babies came from. I was in the bathtub, playing with the toothbrush people. As opposed to at the table, playing with the silverware people — the butter knife father, the soup spoon mother, the dinner fork son, the little spoon daughter, and on holidays, the pickle fork dog. The question concerning babies just sort of popped out, like an afterthought, or a baby. Instantly the air in the bathroom changed, you could cut it with a toothbrush. My mother paused, and in a voice quite unlike the one she'd been using, she told me babies were a gift God gave you when you'd been very very good, as opposed to very very bad, just look at Cookie Flann. For years afterward I was terrified of attracting God's attention by being too good, which might explain a lot of things.

Then there was the time I oh-so-casually asked this same mother some vague question having to do with "down there." Only this time she was moving around my bedroom putting me to bed and stopped dead in her tracks as if she'd suddenly been electrocuted. You could practically smell the flesh burning. Only it was my flesh, or would be, if I didn't mend my ways.

Meanwhile, back on the star-shot freeway, I gathered my wits.

"Um ... " I began, but my daughter cut me off.

"Mom, are you gonna talk about ... all *that*?"

"No," I said. "I mean *yes*," I said. "I mean *why*?" I said.

"Well, I already ... you know ... *know* about all that," she said. "It creeps me out."

"GOOD!!" I shouted, a little too energetically. My voice

reverberated off the side panels. "Keep that thought till you're thirty."

"Mo-*om*," she said, "you *al*ways say the same thing whenever we talk about this." I could feel her eyes rolling around in their sockets.

I drove. The car sped onward through the darkness, as cars are wont to do. After a while Venus appeared in the rearview mirror, followed closely by the moon.

"Hey, remember the eclipse?" I said.

"So what *is* it?" she said.

"When the earth gets between the sun and the moon."

"A *boner*," she said, "what's a *boner*?"

"Hey, isn't that the Big Dipper?" I said.

"Mo-*om*!"

Three beats.

"Do you *really* want to know?" I said, which was unquestionably the most moronic thing I could say, but what the fuck, it's what I said.

"Yes," she said, "I do."

So I told her.

How do parents make it through these minefields? Carefully, in single file. Somehow, as per usual, by the time I was finished, we were laughing hysterically. Both of us. We were hiccuping. Hyperventilating. We were out of control, tears were falling, we had to pee. We'd stop, catch our breath, start again. This went on for forty miles.

Thank God I'm an excellent driver.

When we finally crested that last long hill where the lights of the town suddenly ejaculate out across the landscape, we were limp with exhaustion. By then I was thinking maybe I might work up a routine, you know, like stand-up. A sort of alternative sex education kind of thing, maybe take it on the road. I could start with Boners, move on to The Act Itself, spend some time with that old standby the Egg-and-Sperm, morph into the ever-popular Birth Control and Safe Sex, followed closely by the *coup de grace*, Masturbation, the ultimate safe sex.

I won't hold my breath for the PTA Seal of Approval.

So far my daughter and I have only made it as far as Birth Control and Safe Sex. We can't seem to get any further, we get too loony tunes. This last time maybe that old devil moon had something to do with it, the way it affects tides, menstrual cycles, shit like that. At the rate we're going, who knows when we'll make it to Masturbation. Hopefully not anytime soon. Still, I should google when the next lunar eclipse is. You never know.

TALKING TO DONKEYS ON THE
CHEMIN

Le Bain

In the beginning was the wine. The free wine. We're doing
550 mph, 35,000 feet above the Atlantic, the flight atten-
dants are pouring barrels of the stuff. To keep us sloshed for
eight hours while we chase the sun across the top of the world.

There's Greenland! There's Ireland! Unscrew another one,
s'il vous plait!

Next thing you know I'm in a bathtub in the south of
France, reading. It's 4 a.m. French time. It's always 4 a.m.
French time. Middle of the afternoon, heart of the evening,
anywhere in the world, trust me, it's 4 a.m. in France.

I'm in the bathtub compliments of jet lag. My husband is
finally making the sounds of sleep in the next room, I don't
want to disturb him. It's a nice bathtub. Clawfoot, deep, cool to
the touch. I've filled it with pillows, and a sea of reading material. Maps, *Vanity Fair*, my Berlitz *French Phrase Book*. I'm in
the zone, baby. Until I see the whites of his eyes in the bathroom doorway, rather, the reds.

We're in a third-floor walk-up garret on the Rue Maguelone just off the Place de Comedie in the historic centre of Montpellier, with twenty-foot ceilings and peeling 19th century wallpaper and a lovely view of an airshaft. But it's a French airshaft. The third floor is actually the fourth floor because the ground floor is actually zero. This is the case with many buildings in France. Our third-or-fourth-floor garret is a place to sleep (dream on!), change clothes, bathe ... not a place to write home about.

Nevertheless, in my cozy clawfoot Barcalounger, I'm jotting notes between bouts of "Essential Phrases for Dining Out" and "Was Bill Clinton on the heart-lung machine too long?":

Premiers Impressions de la France:

1. There are no fat people in France.
2. Everybody speaks French.
3. Jet lag is the eighth plague of Egypt.
4. I'm in a bathtub of pillows ... in France.

Everything in France is so ... French. So ... old. Centuries old. Epochs old. It's all so ... historical. So ... European. This place makes America look like Walmart. Wait a minute, America *is* Walmart. The great democratic experiment with forty-eight rolls of Charmin for $7.99. Approximately 5 euros. Give or take.

Le Chien

The homeless people station themselves about the Place de Comedie and profile, their piercings and tattoos flashing in the Mediterranean sun. They all have multiple dogs. Big, dark, fierce-looking dogs — pit bulls, rottweilers, mastiffs — with fat leather collars attached to fat leather leads attached to their owners' fat leather fists.

Most of these dogs are docile. Sort of. Unlike their

owners, who seem about to commit mayhem momentarily. The French police won't throw a homeless person in jail if he or she has a dog. Thus the packs on every corner. Sometimes the owners get into it with each other. The dogs never seem to.

I'm strolling along the Rue Foch one blazing afternoon, and a woman walking toward me asks if I speak English. How does she know? What gives me away? I wasn't even talking, let alone smiling. That's another thing, the French don't smile. Unlike people from Iowa, who really shouldn't.

In France I might as well have laryngitis. I might as well be speaking in tongues. Everyone should experience this language blackout, for humility's sake. Like reentering earth's atmosphere from space. The three minutes of silence multiplied *ad infinitum.*

One day I'm smart and educated and bursting with vocabulary, the next day I'm George W. Bush. Nobody understands me, or wants to. I'm a toddler, *un bebe,* loose on the streets of a foreign city. Except they're cobbled streets, French streets, and there are dogs everywhere. Which, need I remind anyone, are some of my favorite people on earth.

Oo-la-la! Mon petite cher! Mon beau chien! Je t'aime!

Le Chapeau

We take hundreds of photos, thousands. Digital technology allows us this overindulgence. It's so ... American. And to think I agonized over bringing the 35mm.

In addition to the obligatory gardens, architecture and statuary, we take photos of doors. Knockers. Street signs. Shop windows. Fences. Sidewalk cracks. We take photos of ducks, for godsakes, because they're French ducks. They look just like every mallard I ever knew, except they're French. I imitate a duck quacking in a French accent. This lets me know I haven't had enough wine.

Wine is everywhere, any time, day or night. It's ubiquitous. Everlasting. Eternal. Everyone drinks wine. Even the dogs. Even the babies. It occurs to me the plane I came in on may have crashed into the English Channel, and, unbeknownst to *moi*, I've died and gone to heaven.

There are a few French phrases I commit to memory:

1. *Ou est ...* (fill in the blank)?
2. *Je ne parle pas français.*
3. *Parlez-vous anglais?*
4. *Un verre de vin, s'il vous plaît.*

We get caught in a thunderstorm and scurry back to our garret. A full moon lurks somewhere behind the mayhem. We spiral up the spiral staircase, lightning lighting our way. The hallway is as black as the inside of a French cow. I think I see a ghost. In the room there's wine, suddenly we remember the television. Being Americans, we feel vindicated.

We channel surf for a while, comprehending nothing. It's all in French, no subtitles. Why would there be? Seconds tick by, minutes, epochs. It must be 4 a.m.

And then, it happens. Like a rainbow after the storm, or winning at Bingo. In living color, some movie from another lifetime, right before our jet-lagged eyes: Brigitte Bardot's ass. There she is, parading around, naked as a baby. Wait a minute, she *is* a baby. With her, in every scene, is a man. Who cares? But for the fact that in every scene, naked or clothed, this man wears a hat, he remains anonymous. A prop. A phantom. He may as well have laryngitis.

It's one of those Sinatra hats, a small fedora. BB periodically removes it from his anonymous head and puts it on her own lovely impossible one, which makes her look ... more naked. She's speaking French. Why wouldn't she be? Throughout the movie, scene after scene, naked or *dans un chapeau*, French words spill from her lovely impossible mouth, eddy down the air, pool along the bottom of the screen. And for once, and for all, we understand perfectly their meaning.

Les Americains

In the square on the Place de Comedie a protest march forms. Drums beat, flags wave, feet move forward. The protesters follow us across the square, past the fountain of the *Trois Graces*, as we pull our luggage over the cobblestones in the noon heat. They're chanting something, we don't know what. It grows louder and louder. We escape down the stairs into the entrance of the underground parking garage, keeping our eyes peeled for *gobelins*.

Au revoir, Montpellier! Merci pour les mémoires!

We're leaving the city for the countryside, dragging our jet lag behind us.

My husband googles a map and leads us into the landscape in our rented Citroen, past fields and vineyards and small copses of cypress trees *a la* Van Gogh. The car is too large, the pedals too small, my husband is a bull in a stick-shift French china closet.

As if we were given this monstrous vehicle because we're Americans.

Americans with their monstrous bodies and their monstrous voices and their monstrous houses and their monstrous cars. Not to mention their monstrous guns. With their endless obsession to sprawl out across all available space until they've got everything covered. As if taking up space were the endgame.

In France, I'm an American. In America, I'm an outsider.

Le Soleil

We drive, from one roundabout to another, keeping an eye on the sun for direction. The sun is ever-present, like the wine, the distant mountains, the sea. Which is out of sight, but here in the air all around us.

One road leads to another and, finally, the village of Sommieres. It takes as long to find our way through the maze of narrow old streets as it did to drive here from the city. But we do, and then, Hotel de l'Orange. A 17th century chateau converted to guesthouse, perched on a hilltop overlooking the town, *cum* courtyard and gardens and rooftop pool and a small *salon* to call our own. *Maison bienvenue!*

We're dazed, exhausted, bewitched. We wander barefoot over the cool tiles, one room to another, memorizing the view at each window, the art on each wall, the path the sunlight will take across the floor each day.

The shopkeeper around the corner on the Rue Emilien Dumas is patient. She smiles at me, corrects my pronunciation, pats my hand. I buy *emmenthal*, which she wraps in white paper, and *pain*, which pokes up from my shopping bag alongside a bottle of *vin rouge*. The only thing missing from my bag is *fleurs*, but they're everywhere around us. Wild on the hillside, cascading off porches and balconies, spilling from every conceivable cranny and container.

Now I will have a new muscle memory: feet moving over cobblestones, eyes bombarded with color, skin washed in sunlight.

There's something about the Mediterranean light.

We buy tomatoes and peaches and six 14-oz. cans of Heineken. Our *Americain* is showing. Beer tends to come in undersized bottles, we've noticed, we score while we can. We schlep it all home to the rooftop garden and settle in beside a chunk of 2,000-year-old Roman stone to watch the something-about-it sun go down behind the distant mountains.

Les Amis

On the walking path up behind the chateau the vines reach for us, they'd waylay us if they could. The *chemin* is a cool green tunnel in the afternoon glare. Butterflies flit between the branches arching overhead. We pass houses camouflaged in foliage, palm trees and pines, an old cemetery, high ironwork gates from centuries past.

Behind one such gate, in a decrepit garden shed, colorful long-necked bottles with teapots balanced atop them are lined along a table. Classical music is playing. No one is around. We stand for minutes, transfixed.

As we walk, we sing — *"Alouette," "Frere Jacques," "Dites-Moi"* — our *Americain* showing.

Then a sudden bright meadow, a rickety fence, and a donkey ambles over and nudges my hand. Her eyes are long-lashed and soft. We talk for a while, rather, *I* talk. She watches me, bats her lashes, flicks her tail. On our return walk, a small horse has joined her. They stand together at the fence and listen politely as I blather on, in a language they don't understand.

After a while we walk away into the green tunnel, the two of them still watching.

At the flea market I purchase a bronze duck, a child's rusted watering can, three bowls carved from a cypress root, a cast iron pig. The pig has a slit for coins, and wings. Soon she is tucked safely into a carry-on, flying back with us across the Atlantic.

At U.S. Customs, one agent calls another over to the X-ray machine. *Hey, Lois, get a load of this!* Lois calls Danny over, who calls Ed over, who looks around for *l'idiot* who has gone all the way to France — arguably one of the art and culture capitals of the known universe — to bring back a 25-lb. cast iron flying pig. *The Angel Pig*, they call it, and shake their heads and wave us through.

But they're smiling. And when was the last time you saw a customs agent smile?

When I was very young I believed my mother was famous. I believed she was famous because she was beautiful, and because she was an artist. A painter, actually.

Whenever my mother was working on a new canvas, our house would fill with the smell of oil paints. The canvasses were large, and resided in a corner of the dinette for weeks on end, like a succession of drive-in movie screens. She preferred landscapes — farmsteads, orchards, rolling hills, forests. Once she began a seascape, but never finished it. At that time in her life, in those early years of her marriage, she'd never actually seen the sea. Only my father had.

Many years later I sat through all seven nights of The War on PBS, glad when it was over, as uncomprehending as I've ever been of anything in my life. I kept looking for my father.

All I have from that time are two snapshots of him, standing with several other shirtless GIs under enormous palm trees in the South Pacific. Someone took the pictures from too great a distance, so that the human figures in them are dwarfed by the trees, which are dwarfed by the sand and the sky. The whole *effect is of unyielding space and insignificance, in black-and-white. Colors traditionally used to suggest the easy answer.*

I can tell from the photos, obscure though they are, that my father is tan. And thin. And handsome. With a shock of blonde hair above a wide white grin. A photo to send home to your mother. Your wife. To someday show your uncomprehending daughter, along with the set of hand-embroidered table linens, the hand-painted sake decanter, when she asks what you did in the War.

Not, "This is where I once was, when these things happened." But rather, "This is how I once looked, before I became your father."

It seems the things my father brought back from the War were all hand done.

My father was one of those who never talked about the War. Of course, he never talked about much of anything. Not to his daughters, anyway. This was the fifties, fathers were more or less seen and not heard. Unless they were pissed off about something. And if he talked to my mother, it was behind closed doors, out of earshot.

I seem to recall my mother telling me that my father had been a medic in the War. I believe this is so, because I remember thinking, when I was very young, that my father was a doctor. He wasn't, any more than my mother was famous.

The summer I was ten, our family traveled to visit relatives in New Jersey. Once there, the kids secured the rec room while the grownups settled out on the patio for R&R. One stifling afternoon, we all piled into the station wagons and drove to the ocean. The turnpike was crowded, waves of heat shimmied up from the asphalt like mirages. The drive was taking too long, the cars had begun to close in, when suddenly we heard it. Faintly at first, then louder, the sound pulled us forward until at last, as we came over a hill, there it was. The water. As far as the eye could see. Farther. My sense of the world changed in an instant, things would never feel quite the same. Now I'd seen something I hadn't seen. I knew something I hadn't known.

Like lying in the backyard some summer night when you're a kid, and looking up at the stars and realizing, for the first time, that you aren't looking at a ceiling. That there is no ceiling. That there's only distance. Only forever. It's a fleeting recognition, too overwhelming for your childbrain to hold onto, and after a moment, the ceiling closes in again. But it happened. You glimpsed it. If only momentarily.

My mother died, unexpectedly, at the cusp of the new millennium, my father less than two years later. Days prior to her death, my mother told me about a dream she'd had. In the dream, my father was driving the old green Ford, from those years just after the War. He was young again, smiling and waving at her from the open window. And this: the car was flying, a few feet above ground level, moving away from her through the air along a white sand beach. The beach went on as far as the eye could see, and eventually the car, with its waving hand, disappeared into that distant place where the sand meets the water meets the sky.

Here's what I picture: an open car window, a long tan arm, a shock of blonde hair above a wide white grin.

My mother's unfinished seascape was the last she ever worked on. I still have one of her paintings from that time when I thought she was famous. I still have my childhood recollection of the singular smell of oil paints drifting through a three-bedroom rambler in the North Country. I don't know what became of that last canvas, with those broad brushstrokes in faint washes of blue, a background waiting to be revealed. Perhaps finally seeing the ocean altered something for my mother. Perhaps it became one of those experiences which is ultimately so overwhelming, so breathtaking, we're left mute in the face of it. All we have is memory.

When I was growing up, every Thanksgiving, every Christmas, every Easter my mother would lay out the hand-embroidered table linens from the Philippines. But they had grown so precious, so beyond the everyday, that we were wary of them. Instead, more ordinary linens were laid on top of them, and these were the ones we used. Regardless of this, and in spite of the array of special dishes and the sheer amount of food, we always ate more carefully on holidays. As if something were at stake. As if it were up to us to preserve it. Whether or not we understood exactly what it was.

HOUSE BY HOUSE

My mother blamed the rugs at Kmart. That's what she told me, three days before she died

"It was those rugs," she said. "I had to go out to the parking lot to escape the fumes."

That's where my aunt found her, standing by the Buick, staring off into the distance at the sun sinking into the ore dumps.

I think she knew, in that way my mother often seemed to know. When it came to my mother's acclaimed clairvoyance, I have to admit, sometimes she was right on the money.

Like when the neighbor across the street fell off a Euclid at the mine and broke his neck. My mother dreamt it the night before. In the dream this neighbor appeared to her, out of the blue, and gave her a black rose. Even as she was telling me about it the next morning as I sat bleary-eyed over my Wheaties at the dinette table, we watched the neighbor's wife come screaming out of their side door and run across the lawn in her pink babydoll pajamas.

The dead neighbor had been one of my mother's many

suitors in high school, but she'd dumped them all to get on a train for San Antonio and my father. My mother told the story of how some boy stood crying on the platform, begging her to reconsider, as the train pulled out of the station. This was War Time, my father had been drafted. But War or no War, San Antonio must've looked like the Emerald City compared to the hardscrabble mining town where my mother grew up.

That boy on the platform eventually married a girl from a neighboring town, and they moved into a house across the street from us, an idyll which ended when he took a nosedive off that Euclid. I used to imagine how I'd have turned out if he'd been my father instead. Better hair, not much gray matter beneath it.

My mother had a major head of hair, which none of her daughters inherited. She was a brunette, with a streak of gray a mile wide by the time she was seventeen. As if she was marked. And maybe she was. She read tea leaves, dreamt dreams, dispersed clouds, taught her sisters and cousins and later a few bridge ladies and neighbors' wives to play Table Up, and was occasionally overcome by prophetic visions. Like the time a white bird swooped past the clothesline where she was hanging out sheets, and she knew her uncle had died. Or the time she saw in a teacup that a friend would have an accident, and that friend drove off a bridge into a creek on her way to Ting-Town for a burger.

But my mother's prophecies seemed to stop short when it came to her own family. As if a curtain came down. She did better with distant relatives, long lost boyfriends, the occasional Fuller Brush Man. For instance, if she'd really known about my father, about his temper, his solitude, would she still have gotten on that train? And to be fair, if my father had really known about her, would he have sent her the money for the ticket?

But who ever really knows, about themselves, or anyone else? You lose your footing and fall in love and get sucked into the tornado, and the next thing you know you're tripping down the Yellow Brick Road, and before you can yell *I'm melting!*, you're being pursued by flying monkeys and dodging Winkie Guards at the castle.

My mother was the reigning queen of Little White Lieland, and it was at her little white knees that I was first schooled in the ancient art of embroidering the truth. No intricate cross stitch of the Golden Rule to hang on the kitchen wall for that broad, *nosireebob*. My mother's idea of a sampler was having several different versions of the truth to choose from. Like multiple choice:

"I'm sorry, my daughter can't play with your daughter today because ... " (*choose one*)

A. She isn't feeling well.

B. She has to work on her novel.

C. Her doll died.

These were the options in Little White Lieland. In Honestyland, it was always true or false:

"My daughter can't play with your daughter today because your daughter eats paste." (*T / F*)

My mother wasn't big on the truth, she thought it was over-rated. In her world, learning to lie was an exercise in creativity. It smacked of imagination and depth. Why settle for the mundane when you could have the extraordinary? And learning to lie with aplomb was a rite of passage for girls, right up there with never telling your real age and making sure your lips and nails matched.

My mother did, however, make a distinction between a lie and a little white lie, and her daughters were weaned on the latter. Khrushchev and people from Kelly Lake lied. People with breeding and manners told little white lies. And a little white lie was not only creative, it was often the kinder choice, the classic example being:

"That dress looks like sausage casing on you." ... *versus* ... "My, what a nice color!"

So when I casually alter my answers on the questionnaire in the doctor's office regarding the number of alcoholic drinks I consume on a weekly basis, I'm defaulting to an instinct buried deep in my marrow. Why complicate the doctor's busy day any more than necessary? She has bigger fish to fry. What happens in my liver, stays in my liver.

Plus, I want to present myself well, it's what people with breeding and manners do. How would it look to admit I fell out of an outhouse in a drunken stupor and cracked a rib? After all, I'm a direct descendant of the royal house of Norway. At least, that's what Mother always said.

My mother grew up poor during the Depression, in an iron mining town on the edge of the wilderness in the far north of north. A place that genuflected to all things human and male and tended to put females of any species into the category of game animals, which far-outnumbered humans in that corner of the planet. If it moved, you shot it, and worried about classification later.

My grandfather was a handsome rogue, my grandmother a beauty, and no one could decide which of their four daughters was most lovely. Their lives were defined by Relief, odd jobs, the kindness of strangers, and midnight moves from one situation to another when the rent came due. When worse came to worse, my grandfather would disappear for long stretches up into the Canadian bush and return laden with the pelts of dead fur-bearers, which he'd stretch out across the scanty household furniture to dry. That memory of waking up to the odor of wildness and death in the air stayed with my mother.

In spite of being poor they were not poorly raised, thanks to my long-suffering grandmother, who believed in books, art, music, baking, and a white-glove cleanliness no matter how humble the home. When most of her peers resembled punched-down bread dough, my grandmother stood out. My grandfather was a different story. To hear my mother tell it, his daughters adored him, but it was a loyalty which finally faltered when he fathered a fifth lovely daughter, on whom he doted, born to a long-time mistress, and only two years younger than I.

My grandmother had wised up about my grandfather long before this final heartbreak. After years of lies, broken promises, and romantic treachery, she'd finally kicked him out, but not until he'd tried to run her down with the '39 Buick while their two youngest daughters screamed bloody murder in the backseat.

My grandfather eventually became a car salesman, a skill some believed he'd acquired over many decades of selling my grandmother a bill of goods. My grandmother got a divorce, unheard of in those days, and a job working as a secretary for the mine, even more unheard of. She remarried, divorced, married again, three times, forever cementing her status as pariah in that small redneck town, such that the good Catholic ladies crossed to the other side of the street whenever they saw my grandmother coming.

I grew up with the fifth sister, the scandal, the skeleton, in that same town. I was aware of her, but unaware of our connection. It was the fifties, then the sixties, secrets were kept well hidden, lips well sealed. But I put two and two together when she showed up at my grandfather's funeral. I was twenty, she was eighteen. I was sitting in the small chapel waiting for the service to begin when someone entered quietly and sat in the back row. I glanced over my shoulder and mistook her for one of my aunts. Turns out I wasn't mistaken.

* * *

My aunt has a boyfriend. My cousin called to give me the news.

"My mom has a boyfriend," she said.

"Yeah, but does she know she has a boyfriend?" I said.

"Well, the boyfriend knows," she said, "that works for me." And we had celebratory phone cocktails in honor of this development.

When my husband heard about my aunt's boyfriend, he breathed a sigh of relief.

"There's hope for me yet," he said, watching me out of the corner of his eye.

My aunt has Alzheimer's. Now, apparently, she also has a boyfriend. I'm not surprised, my aunt's the hottest number in the Home. The new guy took one look and made his move. My aunt can't remember what day it is, or the names of her children, but she recognized a move when she saw one.

My grandmother also had Alzheimer's, back when they called it senile. She spent her last days in a Home on the Range, where a guy in the next room laid under his bed all day thinking he was fixing his car. The last time I saw my grandmother, I pushed her through the hallways in her wheelchair while she waved the queen wave at passersby like a benediction. My grandmother had no idea where she was, or who I was, but she recognized a parade when she saw one.

You might say I'm descended from a long line of hot numbers, the operative word being descended. In my case the apple not only fell far from the tree, it rolled out of the orchard. Whereas my mother and her sisters and their mother and her sisters laid in their various cribs and cradles instinctively giving tiny queen waves, I lay in mine instinctively giving the tiny finger. Genetic mutation at work. My mother's idea of mutation was to switch to the other hand when one's wrist hurt from waving.

My husband doesn't wave, he watches. Me. But not in the way he used to. In those days, he couldn't stop looking at me. These days, he's looking for signs. Of impending senility, the old genetic crapshoot, the long road to oblivion. *Has she taken another step down that long road to oblivion? or is she just shit-faced?* My mother was probably never shit-faced, not once, in her life. I try not to hold that against her. And she was on her own road when she died, her brain intact, working just the way it always had. I try not to hold that against her, either.

The last time I saw my mother she was standing outside her house, under a streetlight, under a full moon. I glanced in the rearview mirror as I drove away, and she was waving.

During the time my husband and I lived in the woods, I set out for a walk one morning and heard someone call my name. It was spring. I was alone on the path to the river, surrounded by budding trees and pussywillows and a ground cover of deer scat. The voice sounded like one of my aunts, who all sounded alike. I hadn't seen any of my aunts in several years, not since the last wedding. Those were the days of last weddings, these are the days of first funerals.

Six months earlier the Halloween Storm had buried our little corner of the world in thirty-six inches of snow. The Storm of the Century, they called it, and what followed was the harshest winter the North Country had seen in many decades.

Snow so deep, so unnavigable, so silencing, it spread across the landscape like a shroud. Everywhere deer by the thousands were dying on their feet, unable to move, only their heads and necks visible above the unending white.

I spent the better part of an arts grant feeding deer that winter, and would wake each morning to find dozens of them standing motionless among the trees — in their so-called green barn — watching the house, blinking and waiting, in a state of walking-hibernation.

When spring finally came, I went for a walk, and heard my name. The snow was fast disappearing, the air was new, and the small herd of deer I'd kept alive for five long brutal months had vanished back into the woods, leaving behind the evidence of their having been.

My mother died peacefully, in her bed, in her sleep, her ubiquitous radio tucked up next to her ear like a walkie-talkie. It was October.

After drifting around the country for a while, with a years-long stay in Southern California, my parents had returned to the old hometown and bought a small house, their last. My husband drove me and the dog up, and we sat in the car outside the house, beneath the waning moon, while I worked up the courage to go inside. Eventually I did, and the dog kept watch at the guest room door that night while I tried unsuccessfully to sleep.

In the morning I went into my mother's bedroom, into her closet, where I found myself surrounded by her clothes like so many apparitions. I'd been told by the funeral director to pick out something for her to wear, who'd also told me "don't bother with shoes." *Why bother with anything*, I was thinking, *she's dead, jack*. The Funeral Director's name was Steve, not Jack.

I'd liked Patrick for a boy, Jacqueline for a girl. This was at the time of the second ectopic, though we didn't yet know. We were still living in the woods by the river, and my mother was staying with us. Later, when I came home from the hospital, the first thing I noticed as my husband pulled into our long driveway was that my mother had moved one of the lamps in the house. Because, she told me, one should always leave a light burning in the window, just in case.

I'll always think of them, Jacqueline and Patrick, microscopic bundles of rapidly dividing cells on their way to somewhere. But no sooner had the train started gathering speed than suddenly they were gone. Just like that. First one, then the other, left behind by the side of the tracks. In the woods, in the green barn, like lost luggage.

My mother grew up next to the tracks, next to the mine, and at bedtime she would tell us stories from her childhood. She didn't have to invent things, make things up — a habit she developed as my sisters and I got older — because the real stories were good enough. Intrigue, dark and stormy nights, mysterious strangers, ration boxes.

One of my favorites was how my grandmother used to listen for the ore trains, then send my mother and her sisters down to the tracks to get coal. It had to be dark so the watchman wouldn't see, and in winter it was dark by late afternoon. My mother and her sisters and the other kids sent on the same mission would run through the snow alongside the tracks, scooping up coal as it fell from the slow-moving train. Sometimes a kind engineer would throw a few shovelfuls through the open door for the runners to catch in their coats, which they held outstretched in front of them like nets.

At one point the entire town was moved south, house by

house, to make more room for the mine. A practice still taking place years later.

One of my earliest memories is of sitting on a curb between my mother and father, eating a sandwich, watching a house pass by. Like a train, or a parade. I remember peering through the shutters between bites of egg salad, looking for a waving hand, waiting for a glimpse of the people who lived inside.

I wonder where that house is now. Who lives inside. If they ever leave a light burning in the window, just in case.

CATCH AND RELEASE

My cat takes saunas. Thank God for cats.
When you've had a bad day, it's nice to come
home to a cat. Cats don't give a shit. Dogs sense immediately
that you've had a bad day and start groveling. Meanwhile,
you've been groveling all day, enough already, you need a beer.

A cat, on the other hand, locks eyes with you as soon as the
door opens, engaging you in a staredown that will last until one
or the other of you figures out what the cat wants. *Food? treat?
litterbox hasn't been scooped since the midterm elections?* Even
the cat doesn't know.

Accomplished hypnotists, cats will eventually release you
from these recurrent trances with one long blink. By then
you've forgotten all about your lousy day. In fact, you've
forgotten who you are, where you've been, where you're going,
why you're standing stupefied in this vaguely familiar
mudroom staring at a cat.

Dogs invented the term "separation anxiety." When you
leave the house, whether to take out the garbage or go to
France, a dog calls its therapist. A cat couldn't care less where

the hell you're going or if you're ever coming back, just leave the computer on.

When I'm in the sauna, the cat scratches on the sauna door and bellyaches until I let her in, then stretches out on the lower bench and glares at me. I'm listening to the radio, which she disapproves of, preferring the sound of her own being. She continues to glare until I rise like a parboiled phoenix and turn off the radio, at which point she gives me one long blink and starts to purr.

So much for *Talk of the Nation*. The cat particularly disapproves of NPR, which I listen to religiously, even in the sauna. And speaking of religion.

The Lutherans had lutefisk today. You could smell it in Canada.

I'm talking about the church where I work. I just happen to teach at a preschool that happens to be annexed to a church where, though I remain as committed a leftist-boho-pagan as ever, I happen to be surrounded by Lutherans on a daily basis. Today I saw more Lutherans in one afternoon than your shrink would consider advisable. Lutherans absorbed all available parking in a six-block radius, then lined up three deep at the sanctuary door, murmuring softly in their Norwegian sweaters. The line snaked around the parking lot like an intestine.

God help us, if there is one. These days only a church would have the balls to serve lutefisk. And I alone was there to bear witness, a former Lutheran hiding behind my piercings and tattoos. Unlike Catholics, Lutherans don't lapse. They just shift their weight to the other foot.

I grew up Lutheran, though we were fair-weather Lutherans at best. My mother, being Norwegian, was congenitally Lutheran, she had no choice. My father, being Finnish —

it was a mixed marriage — was descended from a long line of communist hermits, he couldn't care less. My father's idea of God was the Sunday paper, a pot of coffee, a box of sweet rolls, and a La Palina. And the women out of the house, at church. Being the father of three girls and the husband of a Norwegian, he craved solitude like a drug.

Every Christmas my mother force-fed us lutefisk as if our identities were in peril. She tried to hide it behind the scalloped potatoes and peas, but we knew. Anyone with a functioning nasal passage knew. My father actually liked lutefisk, but then, being Finnish, he could eat tin if it was boiled long enough. We choked the stuff down with our eyes on the prize: the mountain of gaily wrapped packages piled beneath the tinseled balsam. That's another thing, it had to be a balsam. Pines were for Swedes and heathens, sometimes one and the same.

One of my aunts cooked lutefisk once and it disappeared. Like a miracle. She opened the oven door, and *voila!* nothing was there. Not being known for her culinary skills, she'd left it in too long. A couple of hours, as I recall. My uncle doesn't know how close he came. My uncle was Italian, he made wine in the basement and collected cuckoo clocks. It was a mixed marriage.

Growing up, my best friends were always Catholic. Even back then I knew: Lutherans were boring. I'd look in the mirror and pray for eyebrows. I guess I prayed to Jesus, but my faith was pretty much the size of a mustard seed. I mean, it never got any bigger, and eventually *voila!* it disappeared altogether. Like my aunt's lutefisk. Now I know why she married my uncle, it gave her life substance. Unlike lutefisk, which has none.

Meanwhile, the dog has me figured before I'm through the door. She hangs up on her therapist and falls over in a swoon, tongue lolling out the side of her mouth onto the carpet like toilet paper. The cat is nowhere to be seen.

Discarding various items from my person, I stagger across the room in the general direction of the refrigerator, where I reach for a beer and tilt my head back and *voila!* there she is, perched atop the appliance like the raven in the poem, locked in a staredown: The Cat.

Weak and weary though I am, I ponder: the cat is not so much a raven as a ... gargoyle? No, that's not it, she's ... St. Francis? the Sheriff of Nottingham? Martin Luther? the new prepubescent mentally unstable director of the preschool where I teach??

But by now it doesn't matter. I've forgotten all about my lousy day, and whatever it is about me that made it lousy in the first place, and the fact that I smell like the bottom of a barrel of cod cured in lye. I stand in the middle of the vaguely familiar kitchen and raise my beer in a toast.

"Nevermore!" I toast, and the cat gives me one long blink and starts to purr.

* * *

The preschoolers have a new game. The girls, that is. I discovered it yesterday.

There I am, circling the room, cleaning up after the art project — a complicated process involving packing peanuts and Popsicle sticks — when I notice a gaggle of girls playing quietly in the housekeeping corner, quietly being the operative word. When you teach preschool, decibel levels below Airbus A330 are always a welcome reprieve.

When next I pass this little scene of domestic bliss, I overhear one of the girls — let's call her Lizzie — cooing softly to the baby in her arms,

"Let's get you into the bath, sweetie."

Smug in the knowledge of my superior abilities with this endearing age group — who knew?! — I continue circling in search of errant boys planning lord-knows-what icky boyish mischief, ready to infiltrate and disband the mini terrorists before the deal goes down.

On my third pass, I notice that all the babies in the house-keeping corner have been stripped naked and placed in various bathing receptacles, including the sink, and now Lizzie is stuffing three of them into the top-loading washer and closing the lid.

"There, there," she coos, "don't be afraid, we have to do this."

I pause in my rounds. Now Lizzie is joined by let's-call-her Rachel, who peers intently at the front of the washer and announces with concern that, *uh-oh*, blood is dripping between the cracks.

"Oh dear," sighs Lizzie, "there's no more towels."

I never do find out why the babies are bleeding, only that they are. *All* of them. *Every single one.* Apparently the entire preschool is flowing with blood. It has to be, given the number of bodies lying about. Lizzie has no explanation for the blood-bath other than to say with eye-rolling exasperation that they're bleeding from "*every*where" and it happens "*all* the time." She motions for me to bend down.

"That's why they're naked," she whispers into my ear in hot little puffs, "so their clothes don't get all bloody."

Can't argue with that.

I don't know, maybe it's a new take on that old standby, playing doctor. Why bother with sex? Let's have carnage, with its endless possibilities.

. . .

I remember playing doctor one Christmas Day long ago. Santa had given me a doctor kit, and naturally I stuck the plastic thermometer in my cousin's ear. He ended up in Emergency. I ended up banished to the rec room with a spanking and no dessert, until my old Finnish grandma snuck down with a plate of mincemeat pie and a cigarette. The cigarette was for her, though I wouldn't put it past her to have offered me a drag.

My grandma was forty when she gave birth for the first and only time, to a son, my father. She was the quintessential Old School Grandma — long hair rolled in a bun, wire-rim glasses, black lace-up shoes, shapeless housedress. She tucked hankies into the sleeves of her sweaters and spoke Finnish, with a few English words thrown in to show off. She lived in a single-room-bathroom-down-the-hall in a turn-of-the-century brownstone in the old port city on The Big Lake, with a dozen or so other old widowed Finnish ladies, whom she'd known since first arriving in America with her sister at the tender age of twenty.

My grandma would often come to stay with us "to help my mother." But she'd no sooner have her black cloth coat and felt hat off, than she'd ferret out me and my sisters and tuck herself into our lives for the duration. She'd play board games with us for hours, though she barely knew what was going on. She'd roll jacks with us, watch us jump rope, help with our roller skate keys, wait patiently at the end of the driveway as we circled the block, again and again, on our bikes. She loved for us to read to her. I think she was dumbfounded to know she had grandchildren — *girls!* — who ran around speaking English like there was no tomorrow. She'd nod and grin and pat our heads with her large strong hands, jabbering away in a language we didn't know but somehow understood.

And she had her ways.

She loved her cigarettes, Lucky Strike nonfilters. I can still see the small white pack with the red bullseye tucked into the pocket of her cotton bib apron. My parents had forbidden her to smoke in the house, so she'd pace up and down the driveway, smoking and muttering, like a convict. She'd walk us kids to the market or the playground or to school in the morning, chainsmoking all the way, ashing into the palm of her hand. In winter, when it was too cold to step outside, she'd sneak to a far corner of the basement and blow smoke out the open window well screen. This drove my father crazy, and they'd start arguing back and forth in Finnish until my mother quietly closed the basement door and looked around for something to dust or straighten.

One Saturday, during one of my grandma's visits, my parents left her to watch the kids while they ran errands. It was winter, and we spent the morning indoors, playing board games, rolling jacks, reading aloud. When it came time for lunch, my grandma bundled us up like Laplanders, and we all trudged through the snow up to First Avenue, where she tossed her Lucky in a snowbank, stuck out her thumb, and hitched us a ride uptown. She was saving bus money, she later explained to my father. We had tuna salad sandwiches and strawberry sodas at Woolworth's counter, then she hitched us a ride back home again. Where my father was waiting.

I remember a story about a friend of my grandma's from the Old Country who'd also emigrated to the New World. The family lived for a while on a farm in Ontario, where the children attended a country school. The students were forbidden to speak Finnish inside the school grounds, which were surrounded on all sides by a tall wrought iron fence. So they'd lie on the ground inside the fence, their heads poking out between the pickets, and jabber away in their native tongue like there was no tomorrow.

We were birds of a feather, my old grandma and I, stuck in

the middle of a family whose language and customs we didn't quite get the hang of. Whenever I visited the second-floor-walkup in the old port city where she lived, she'd let me suck my thumb to my heart's content while she stood watch at the open doorway, puffing away on a Lucky. At the first sound of my father's footfall on the staircase, she'd give a signal, and out would come my cork, as my parents called it.

There I am, at the tender age of seven, in the early stages of a lifelong oral fixation.

Although having taught preschool these past few years, not to mention parented the girl who would be my daughter, I can tell you, no age is tender. They're all tough. Ask my old grandma, if she were still here. Ask my daughter, who is.

My daughter came home from school the other day to find a big black bird flying around inside the house. A starling, as it happens, and it's happened before. They nest in the eaves outside her bedroom on the second floor of our 100-year-old house and occasionally find their way down the chimney into the unused fireplace in the room next to hers.

The 100-year-old floorboards shudder as she drops her 100-lb. backpack, which in turn startles the starling, who swears a bluestreak and flies into another room, dripping blood. The dog is oblivious to all this, as dogs are wont, being more interested in the amalgam of encyclopedic scents my daughter has brought back from another stinky day in middle school. Meanwhile, the cat thinks she's won Publisher's Clearing House.

My husband, having been summoned by a frantic text message from his daughter, arrives home to find the bird barricaded in the TV room, flapping wildly from one sunlit window to the other, back and forth across the hopeful smiling faces of twenty Alaskan bachelors on *Oprah*. My husband manages somehow to capture the wretched creature in an empty Corona box (in our house, they're always empty), and having determined that its foot is injured — either from the trip down the chimney or a close call with the cat — he finally releases it out into the yard, where it swears one last time, shits for good measure, and flies off into the shining universe.

My daughter, meanwhile, has escaped to gymnastics practice, and my husband spends the rest of *Oprah* and all of *Dr. Phil* cleaning bird blood from countless surfaces in our 100-year-old house, which flows with the stuff in much the same way I imagine the preschool would, if Lizzie and Rachel had their druthers. Although, unlike the starling situation, baby *shit* does not appear to be a component of Lizzie's and Rachel's bloody play, so far as I can tell.

Which, incidentally, was one of my father's favorite adjectives (*the bloody traffic! the bloody election! the bloody fish aren't bloody biting!*), taking the place of swear words, it would seem, in his I'm-a-good-father lexicon. I'll lay odds his old mother swore, no doubt prolifically, but in Finnish, so no one understood. Further evidence of our being from the same flock, she and I, the difference being my talent in that direction has always been delivered in plain English.

For instance, my reaction upon hearing the starling story from my husband:

"The poor fucking thing," I reacted, setting down an empty Corona bottle. "When are you gonna fix that fucking fireplace flue?"

Alliteration at its fucking best.

And then there's metaphor. Because literature down through the ages loves a big black bird.

There we are, my husband and I, sitting before a crackling fire last evening, exchanging our bloody stories. I look around the living room, at the graceful coved ceiling, the towering mantel, the surrounding oaken woodwork, and I can't help but see the symbolism in that big black bird. Caught within the walls of this old house, wanting desperately to escape, flailing blindly toward the light.

And I can't help but recognize my daughter in that struggle, caught within the walls of this old house, wanting desperately to escape, flailing blindly toward the light. The light of her own future. Away from the past, away from us, somewhere off into the shining universe.

CALLING IT A NIGHT

A n old friend and I were having a phone cocktail the other night, playing catch up after a long absence.

"It could be worse," I said. "We could be in an iron lung."

I'd recently watched a PBS show about Polio. Remember Polio? Whatever happened to Polio? If you got Polio, you skipped school for a couple of years and talked to your mother in a mirror attached to your iron lung.

"Hey, Mom," you'd say, "bring me some more ice cream!"

The girls in an iron lung always had bows in their hair. The boys had freckles. The doctors and nurses were dressed in white, the nurses had white Chinese takeout cartons on their heads. All these white people stood around the iron lung smiling and chatting, as if it were the latest time-saver from Electrolux:

"Now you can get dinner on the table while your son/daughter continues breathing in the next room!"

Polio was second only to the Bomb as the ultimate parental deterrent.

"If you (choose one) *step foot in a pool hall / don't eat those*

brussels sprouts / leave the house in that outfit ... you'll get Polio!"

Whereas the Bomb was all about guilt (*"You'll be sorry you used that tone with me when they drop the Bomb!"*), Polio was all about consequences. If you didn't do A, then B would happen. You had control over the thing. Not so with the Bomb. When it came to the Bomb, it wasn't up to you. It was up to Them. Someone or something else was the Decider.

The aforementioned PBS show ended happily-ever-after, with old black-and-white footage of smiling kids eagerly lining up to get their Polio shots. Everything went swimmingly. The smiling doctors brandished their two-foot syringes and the grateful kids took it on the chin — rather, the arm — with nary a tear.

I don't know in what suburb of Stepford those films were shot. It certainly wasn't my neck of the woods.

I remember standing in line for a Polio shot at Greenhaven Elementary while kids a few miles ahead of me screamed and fainted. Inch by inch we inched forward, toward our bloody destiny, our young lives flashing before us. (*"Why oh why did I hide that piece of liver in the sansevieria?" "Why oh why did I look at that page in* National Geographic *so many times?" "Why oh why did I call my sister a poopy poop?"*) At one point I might have made a dash for it, only to be hauled back into line by the long hairy arm of the Principal, Mrs. Whitwell.

I never was any good with needles.

Once I had to be pulled from the Gay Blades Skating Show because my cheek swelled to the size of a bocce ball. Turns out it was an abscess. I refused to open my mouth at the emergency midnight dental appointment my mother hastily arranged, and eventually the dentist packed up his novocaine and his whiskey-breath and went home. This was the dentist who shot off three fingers of his right hand cleaning his deer rifle, as opposed to the one who went to prison for filling kids' perfectly healthy teeth.

I don't make this shit up, I grew up on the Range.

My phone cocktail friend came of age in a more civilized environment. Her next-door neighbors had a bomb shelter. She and the neighbors' daughter used to sneak down into the bomb shelter and count the canned goods that lined the shelves. She tried to be extra nice to this girl, she said, because you never knew.

"Remember that *Twilight Zone* where the people build a bomb shelter and then they think the Bomb has dropped and then all the neighbors break into the bomb shelter and then everybody starts hitting everybody with baseball bats and then it turns out it wasn't the Bomb after all?" I ask my friend on the phone between swills of pinot grigio.

The aforementioned town where I grew up had a bomb shelter — *one* bomb shelter — which soon became a tourist attraction. Not that the homeowners let anyone through. People just lined up out on the sidewalk and pointed toward the backyard and imagined the bomb shelter down there beneath the sod. By the time I was in high school, the Bomb's glory days were over, and the once-popular tourist attraction became a party hangout for the homeowner's wasted son and fifty of his closest friends.

"So it could be worse," I say. "We could be *in* an iron lung *in* a bomb shelter."

"With *no* drugs," says my friend.

At this point my daughter hollers up the stairs, *You're taking too long! What're you doing up there anyway? I need you to quiz me on the female reproductive system!*

I tell this to my friend, who happens to be a nurse. She wasn't a nurse when I knew her down in The City. She turned into a nurse after I moved away, and I turned into a has-been.

That was twenty years ago. Before I moved away, we used to do drugs together and hang out. But never in a bomb shelter.

"I don't think I've ever even been *in* a bomb shelter," I say.

"Let alone an iron lung," she says.

We have one more for the road, then call it a night and hang up.

My daughter pronounces it "FALL-o-PEE-in-tube" and I start giggling and she gets miffed and then she says, *You've been laughing all night up there what's so funny anyway?* and so I tell her and then she says, *That's not funny how would you like it if you had Polio?* and of course she's right and then she says, *What is Polio anyway?* and now I start laughing even harder and I can't help it and I'm out of control and I'm a bad bad mother and I'm a bad bad person and I'm going to hell.

In a handbasket.

Or maybe an iron lung.

Or maybe a bomb shelter.

* * *

If you want to feel really good about yourself, go to a party where the median age is seventy-three. I was a hit. I was the hottest number there.

Guys kept asking about the chick in the tight jeans with legs up to her neck. It helps if you're wearing really tall shoes. A woman I know — she's in my general age range, only shorter — periodically stopped by to whisper updates into my shoulder.

"That guy leaning against the door? He's the head of some department, I forget which. He wants to know who the new girl is."

I glance up. The guy looks like he's using the door to keep from tipping over. He raises his eyebrows in my direction. I lower my gaze, whisper into my new friend's hair.

"I hope they rented a defibrillator along with the party trays."

I sip my wine. Who am I kidding? I swill it. My age-bracket informant sweeps past again.

"That bunch over by the fireplace? They want to know if you're married."

I study the bunch in question, who appear to be studying the painting above the mantel. They keep glancing at me. Just then my husband walks up.

"You're so tall tonight," he says, and he should know.

"It's the platforms," I say. "How's about a little more vino?"

He takes my glass and walks off. I'm alone, without a prop. My arms hang uselessly by my sides. These are the times I wish I still smoked. I pretend to search through my pockets for something, I can hardly get my fingers in.

"What're you looking for?" says my husband, returning, holding out my glass.

"Stage business," I say. "Did they run out of white?"

"No-o," he says. "I filled it to a polite level."

"Speaking of polite," I say, "where's the Little Girls'?"

I move across the room carefully — wouldn't want to destroy anyone's fantasy by falling off my shoes — and I can feel it, something I haven't felt for some time: I'm being watched. Like a friend of mine said a couple decades ago, *You know you're over the hill when construction workers stop paying attention.* I used to hate it when they whistled. Now I'd give my eyeteeth to disrupt one last road project.

I close the door behind me, check my eyeteeth in the mirror. So far so good. But who looks at the teeth? These guys, that's who. They probably check the teeth first thing.

As I re-enter the living room, I can almost hear the snare drum.

"What's the matter with you?" asks my husband.

"I'm smiling," I say, flashing the pearly whites.

"You *never* smile," says my husband. "Are you drunk?"

I ignore him.

"Oh, look," I say, turning to the left, my best profile. "I seem to have run out again. This time, don't be so polite."

My husband gives me a knowing look. I pretend my earring needs adjustment and scan the room. My new best friend is standing with another group of guys, they're riveted in my direction. She gives me a knowing look. She and my husband should get together and share their knowledge. One of the guys takes off his glasses and puts them in his pocket. Like this helps.

My husband returns with a plate of food and two glasses.

"You missed your calling," I say, "you would've made a stellar waitron."

I knock back a sizeable swill.

"Stellar Waitron," I muse. "Great name for a ... " But I can't think what.

"For a newscaster," says my husband.

"An exotic dancer," say I.

"A mystery writer," says he.

"A department head."

Now I'm picturing a big head sitting on a podium, lecturing. The head is male, of course, with gray hair — no, wait, it's bald — and glasses. I look around the room, seeing only heads. Most of them fit the above description, more or less. I hold up my wine.

"Behold a glass half empty," I say, giving my husband a knowing look.

"Or half full," he responds on cue.

"'The trick is to know which is which,' she said with profundity," I say profoundly.

My husband is staring at me.

"You're the hottest number here," he whispers warmly.

I'm thinking *BFD*, *I'm the* only *number here*, but I keep this thought to myself.

"Who's counting?" I say, and raise my half-filled glass in a toast.

* * *

It's New Year's Eve, I'm at the cabin, the phone rings. It's my husband, calling from a car wash. From inside the car as it's being washed. This is the same husband who called on Labor Day, from a tree in the middle of a clearing in the middle of the wilderness.

It's always the same.

It's Labor Day, I'm at my computer, the phone rings.

"*Hon?*" he screams. "*Are you there? Hon?*"

I'm always here. Where else would I be? I can think of a few places, but it's no use. I don't get around much anymore. Those days are over. *Morte. Kaput.*

My husband, however, does. Get around. He calls from trees and cars. He calls from planes about to take off, planes about to land, planes about to sit on the tarmac for five hours. He emails from cafes in Barcelona and pubs in Scotland. He texts from Amsterdam, Trondheim, Hinckley.

It's August, I'm at the Blues Fest, the phone rings. It's my husband, calling from the parking lot.

"*Hon?*" he screams. "*Are you there? Do you want a beer?*"

"No!" I scream. "*I want a life!*"

I had a life once. It was called the seventies. I even remember parts of it.

What I remember is this: I could move all my worldly possessions from one apartment to another in two carloads.

This was the Chevy Nova era. Before the Mustang era. After the Mazda with the wonky, er, Wankel engine era, the car that sounded like a jet taking off. It sounded like a jet taking off after I accidentally ran over a WRONG WAY sign in the Southtown parking lot on my way to see *The Sting* for the first time. I went back eleven times. Then I got a divorce.

That was a whole different husband.

I met that husband when he keeled over into a plate of spaghetti, asleep. This should've been a clue, but one of my favorite activities at the time was to get stoned and vacuum, who was I to judge. That husband — let's call him the starter — worked for Ma Bell, we had a phone in every room. I'd get stoned and call him from various locations in the house. He'd be hanging off a telephone pole in Anoka County, his mobile would ring. It'd be me calling from the bathroom. I never had much to say, but our house was immaculate.

On Saturdays I'd fire up the hookah and reach for the Pledge. The starter would fire up his Trans Am and reach for the Turtle Wax. He preferred Lambrusco, I favored Thai Stick. I was addicted to Top 40 Classical, he was obsessed with Chicago. It was a mixed marriage. Mostly we watched *Mod Squad* and our parakeet, Stanley. We first came upon Stanley flying happily around Woolworth's, having just escaped prison, and it hit me like a bong rip — the mothering instinct. We'd gone in search of pipe cleaners, and come back parents.

Stanley had full run of the house, flying from room to room, from one ringing phone to another, chattering away. When he got into a bag of Panama Red I'd left on the counter, I played *The Pastoral* for him as he rode it out. When he hitched a ride outside on my toweled head and flew around the hood for a few days, Prokofiev brought him back down. He was fond of eggs and would eat them off my plate, something I found vaguely cannibalistic. When I showered, he'd sit on the curtain rod and sing his little blue heart out. He could say "Fuck you!" and "Far out!," but only I could tell the difference. A chipmunk regularly snuck into the house — we never determined how — and I'd often return to find the two of them, Stanley and the Munk, conversing away from their respective perches.

That was my life: stoned to the gills in a clean clean house where Beethoven and ringing phones competed for available airspace. Good news: I'd wake in the morning and a little blue bird would be nestled beside me on the pillow, running his little yellow beak along my cheek and cooing. Bad news: the starter would be there, too.

Something had to give. It was Chicago. All those horns finally did me in.

One day it's Saturday, the starter's in the bathroom, the phone rings. It's me, calling from California. Remember, I used to get around.

"Don't get me started!" I scream. *"I want a divorce!"*

I flew back from California, packed up my guitar, my piano, my pipe and my mop, and moved to a farmhouse south of the river. It was winter. The farmhouse had inconsistent heat, and I had to leave Stanley behind. I cried and agonized and kissed Stanley good-bye, then dried my tears, and with a bong not a whimper, hightailed it on down the road in my little yellow Mazda into the rest of my life.

After a while the starter acquired a roommate — let's call him the roomie — who also had a parakeet. Can you *believe* that? The starter and the roomie put the new bird (let's call him the usurper) into the cage with Stanley, then proceeded to Turtle Wax their muscle cars and guzzle Lambrusco and groove to Chicago like two peas in a pod. The roomie was also apeshit over Chicago, can you believe *that?*

During this time, Stanley grew anxious. He began eating all the seed in the two seed cups, so as not to leave any for the usurper. He grew fat, and could no longer fly, and waddled about on the carpet while the usurper swooped and soared overhead. Then one bitter day, Stanley keeled over onto the floor of his cage, and died. Just like that. As usual, it was winter. The starter and the roomie didn't know what to do with the body, so they put Stanley in the freezer until spring, when they could give him a proper burial.

I didn't know about any of this until my soon-to-be-ex-sister-in-law called the farmhouse to fill me in. I only had one phone, a party line, which proved to be more entertaining than any or all former phones or husbands put together. By this time I also had a better guitar, a job playing it, a cat, a dog, and a couple of groupies.

I still think about Stanley. I went on to have other guitars, other jobs, other cats, dogs, and groupies, another husband. But I've never had another bird.

I met my true husband — let's call him the keeper — when he was delivering the mail.

Let me explain.

Due to "mailbox inconsistencies," our mail carrier had suspended delivery to the dozen or so apartments in the building where the keeper and I both lived, a converted mansion in the Lake District in the old neighborhood down in The City. With the exception of the keeper, all occupants of said building were female. We regarded our ongoing mail-less state as nothing less than a miracle of good karma, which allowed us to get on with the business of living, *i.e.*, partying our asses off between bouts of quasi-gainful employment.

The keeper, however, solid citizen that he was, complained to the local mail substation. After assuring him that any inconsistencies regarding mailboxes would be taken care of, he was handed a box containing all of the back mail for the entire building. He spent that evening distributing two weeks' worth of letters, bills and free Happy Hour passes to each unit, mine being the last, on the top floor.

Thus was born the legend of the U.S. Male, my husband. The rest is his story.

Fast forward a few decades.

My husband and I are having a party. I'm up on the third floor. I've repaired to the third floor to escape the melee below and blow a doobie out the window, shades of the old days. One of the other partygoers has repaired with me. We're sitting quietly, repairing beside the window, staring at the wall.

Suddenly, the stillness is shattered.

"I wish ... I had a drink ... " says Other Partygoer, "but ... I don't think ... I can move."

"I can move ... my arm ... " I say, and pick up the phone.

"*Hon?*" I whisper. "*Is that you? Can you ... bring ... some wine?*"

Ten seconds later, or maybe it was half an hour, there's a tap on the door. It's my husband, with a tray. He sets it down, raises his eyebrows, retreats.

"Wow ... " says OP, "I've never seen ... anything like that ... before."

"Like what ... before?" I say, moving my hand toward the bottle.

"Like making ... a phone call ... " she says, "to someone ... somewhere ... in the same house."

"Someone who ... brings *drinks*," I say, and pour.

After a few minutes, or maybe it was an hour, I look up. OP is staring at the wall. Not the same wall, a different wall. A wall with a photo on it. A head shot, black and white, just me and the mic and the spotlight and the night.

"Wow ... " she says, "when was that ... taken?"

"The seventies ... " I say. "I used to ... have a life."

OP considers this. She looks around the small cluttered room tucked up under the eaves — my study — where we've been repairing.

After a while, or maybe it was immediately, she lifts her glass.

"Well here's to ... whatever it is ... you have now ... " she says, and we drink to that.

LAST PLACE ON EARTH

You know something's up when you find yourself in Walmart the night before Thanksgiving holding a pumpkin pie. They're on special. You're only in Walmart because the preschool where you teach ran out of those shiny star stickers circa yesteryear, and Walmart is the last place on earth that still carries them.

Christmas is coming, you need all the stars you can get. That's what you tell yourself.

"I'm only in Walmart because it's the last place on earth," you tell yourself.

In your former life Walmart hadn't even made it out of Arkansas yet. But if it had, you wouldn't have been caught dead there. Unlike being caught dead in the Arctic Cold Plunge at the European Health Spa, which has a certain panache.

In your former life you used to have a couple hits of pot and hang out in the Eucalyptus Vapor Room because it gave you visions. You got into the European Health Spa due to an endless supply of free passes, compliments of a friend of yours who had a gig rosemaling coffee tables for one of the owners.

The party ended when your friend ended up in Emergency with blood poisoning from breathing paint thinner. On your last free pass, you breathed eucalyptus until your eyes changed color, then took the Arctic Cold Plunge.

Which proved to be good preparation for the rest of your life.

So there you are in Walmart the night before Thanksgiving with a pie in your hand, and it occurs to you this might be it, you might have been caught dead. You look around at the other shoppers, and now you're worried. You used to stand out like a sore thumb. Now nobody even looks at you. It's like you're one of them. You might as well buy a pink velour tracksuit and start smoking again.

Which gets you thinking about the girls at the preschool where you teach. Not the smoking part, the pink part.

The girls in your class wear pink pink pink, nothing but pink, you're concerned for the future of the country. You hail from the School of Basic Black, your idea of color being blue eyes, which you have, probably thanks to the Eucalyptus Vapor Room. So does Jesus, according to the photo hanging in the hall of the church to which the preschool is annexed, which always pisses you off. You have half a mind to take a water-soluble marker and color Jesus's eyes brown. The other half says take a deep breath and wait for a vision.

Only don't hold that breath.

Each week at the preschool you celebrate another letter of the alphabet, including as many words beginning with that letter as a four-year-old brain can conjure. When you can't conjure any more, the students take over. So there you are, going along without a care in the world, when suddenly, during J week, you forget Jesus. Not that he figured prominently in your lesson plan to begin with. But one of the girls-in-pink reminds you.

"Jar! Jacket! Jellybean! Jugular!" you conjure.

"Jesus!" conjures the pink girl.

Actually, you have nothing against Jesus. You address him regularly, using his full name.

"A goddamn preschool?! Jesus H. Christ! The last place on earth I expected to end the fuck up!"

Later that same day — that is, the day you forgot Jesus — you're slaving away over next week's lesson plan, when you finally have it: a vision. You've been brainstorming the ever-popular "Question of the Week," which figures prominently every Wednesday and features such time-honored queries as "What is your favorite color?" or "Would you rather have broccoli or Cocoa Puffs for dinner?," when you eschew the traditional choices in favor of:

> *Who do you like better?*
> *A. Jesus*
> *B. Santa*

You are beside yourself with self-congratulatory delight. You've just conjured the Question to End All Questions for the preschool set, and you celebrate with a couple hits of Diet Coke and a eucalyptus cough drop.

Which gets you thinking about the Eucalyptus Vapor Room at the European Health Spa, which gets you thinking about the Arctic Cold Plunge, which gets you thinking about how it turned out to be such good preparation for the rest of your life, speaking of which, here you are, teaching in a goddamn preschool at the ass end of nowhere, Jesus H. Christ.

Which reminds you it's J week and you forgot Jesus, which reminds you Christmas is coming, which reminds you to grab another in an endless supply of Post-Its and write "star stickers," unaware that this simple act of reminding will land you several weeks hence in the purgatory of Walmart the night before Thanksgiving, wondering if the party's finally over and you've bought the farm.

Which, it occurs to you, is not unlike ending up in Emergency with blood poisoning from breathing paint thinner, speaking of which, whatever happened to that rosemaling friend of yours anyway? Last you'd heard she'd ended up in Emergency with food poisoning after eating sale-price potato salad from SuperAmerica, and thus you decide, at the last minute, to forgo the pie.

So there I am at Walmart, the last place on earth I expected to be, being of the Target demographic.

There I am, minding my own business, after an emergency run for star stickers and the usual $99-last-minute-must-haves, when this kid working checkout feels a need to share.

This kid is like seven feet tall, tips the scales at a whopping 130, ten pounds of it hair. I hand over my cloth bags, he narrows his eyes behind his glasses and glares down at me.

"You'll have to hold those your*self,*" he says, stuffing a box of Honey Nut Cheerios into a plastic bag.

"Bu-ut ..." I say, "I don't *want* plastic, that's why I brought *these.*"

He sighs audibly, pulls the Cheerios out of the bag, throws the bag into the trash.

"Bu-ut ..." I say, pointing to the discarded bag, "can't you reuse that?"

"Do *you* want to reuse it?" he asks, pushing his bangs aside, reaching toward the trash. Do I detect a wee bit o' attitude here?

"Will it get recycled?" I ask warily, glancing up at him. This time he rolls his eyes.

"No," he says. "I mean, I don't know," he says. By now I'm standing there like Santa Claus holding my bag open as he stuffs shit in. Then he says,

"I don't believe in all that. Global warming and all that. There's no such thing."

I'm taken aback. I can't remember the last time I was taken aback. I didn't expect my day to end with this towering neanderthal at Walmart sweating all over my reusable market bags and sharing his cockamamie beliefs.

"Well *good* for you," I say in my most ironic voice. But the kid's a throwback, he doesn't get irony, let alone in-your-face sarcasm. He pushes his glasses back up and continues sharing.

"I just throw everything away," he shares. "I don't believe in recycling," he shares. Then he shares again, louder, "There's no such thing as global warming!" and wipes his hand across his American flag T-shirt.

Now *I'm* staring. I might even be staring slack-jawed. I can't remember the last time I was slack-jawed.

So there I am at Walmart, staring slack-jawed at this mouth-breathing troglodyte working checkout, to whom I should be gently explaining how his eating habits themselves are part of the problem (there's a bulging McDonald's bag on the floor by his foot), but that would take too long, and anyway he wouldn't listen, and besides, I'm getting this image. I'm thinking of all those guys you read about who flip out and shoot up the workplace or the school or the courtroom or the inlaws' double-wide. I'm thinking this kid could definitely be one of those guys. I'm thinking maybe that's what this kid is reaching for under the counter. I'm thinking this kid could be a shooter.

But does this stop me? This doesn't stop me. I can't remember the last time anything stopped me. I turn to the woman standing behind me in line.

"Don't you just *love* Americans?" I say to her. I have to work *real hard* not to insert a "fucking" somewhere in that sentence.

I stagger out into the parking lot with my overloaded reusable market bags, and it starts to rain. Actually it's a downpour. Actually it's a deluge. I slog through the rising floodwaters toward the ark of my car, and it starts to hail. Pinballs of ice ricochet off my head and collect in the crevices of my overloaded market bags. I can't find my car in the blinding torrent, then my shin finds it for me.

"*Fu-uck!*" I holler. Then I holler again, louder. "*FU-UCK!!*"

I look around, embarrassed. At least I have the wherewithal to be embarrassed. I can't remember the last time I had any wherewithal. But it's zero visibility. I'm alone, abandoned, an island awash in a sea of indifference, being pummeled into oblivion by a random act of climate change.

Finally, inside my car, hail jackhammering overhead, my purchases melting like glaciers around me, I look in the rearview mirror and gasp audibly. My hair is plastered to my head like seaweed, my eyes are black holes of mascara, black streaks run down my cheeks like scars. I look like a caveman!

There's nothing to do but wait it out. (*Note to self: Keep emergency bottle of tequila in glovebox.*) The minutes tick by. Now the windows are fogging up. By the time the storm is over, I've written "!KCUF" a half dozen times on the glass. I wipe the windows with the flat of my hands, look around at the aftermath, and start my engine.

SIX FEET ABOVE

I've got a pitch for a new HBO series:
Childless couple pushing fifty opens their door one
morning to find a baby in a basket on the doorstep. Like Moses.
They take the baby in. If they didn't, they'd be heartless dickwads, not worth the booze it takes to keep them upright. Also,
there'd be no HBO series.

The basket isn't actually a basket. It's an empty Bud case.
The baby isn't actually a baby. It's a four-year-old SoCal gangbanger smuggled into the Witness Protection Program. After a
few rounds of DDT and a butch haircut eradicates the head
lice situation, they buy it new clothes and discover it's a girl.

They call her Moe.

Being a rescue, Moe fits nicely into the household, which is
filled with other rescued creatures. Who am I kidding? Strike
"nicely" from that last sentence. This isn't primetime, this
is HBO.

In the First Season we're introduced to the main characters,
who don't live in a funeral home, but they might as well. There
are no half-embalmed bodies marinating in the basement, but

there might as well be. No one's dead — yet — and no one's gay. Yet. The First Season ends with Moe and one of the other rescues — a puppy who rampages around with its mouth wide open in search of something to dispatch — forming a tentative bond.

In the Second Season, the childless couple — who are no longer childless and have pushed fifty out the door and into the street where it gets run over by a snowplow — are in the throes of an awakening. The dog — who is no longer a puppy — is on a mission to take over as alpha female. Moe is on a mission to take over in general, starting with the household and, after that, the Upper Midwest. Between the two of them, they manage to put the rude into the childless couple's awakening. The season ends with Moe's first day of kindergarten, September 12, 2001.

A nice bit of foreshadowing. Strike "nice."

In the Third Season, the childless couple is now fully awake. Moe — who is no longer a toddler — rampages around with her mouth wide open looking for something to dispatch. The dog — who has given up trying to dispatch the wife, but occasionally casts her a disparaging look — worships submissively at Moe's feet. Moe couldn't care less. She now favors the cat, who, being a cat, couldn't care less. No one could care less than the plecostomus, who watches everything unfold from behind the fake boulder in front of the fake backdrop beneath the fake plants in the 50-gallon aquarium, its home of sixteen years. Generations have come and gone, the pleco has seen it all.

That's the angle! Backstory! Everything from the fish's POV!

The Fourth Season begins with Moe having barricaded herself in her bedroom with the cat, who couldn't care less, and her cell phone — Moe's, not the cat's — with which she issues demands for equipment and supplies from the childless couple, who are no longer awake but wandering around in a sort of somnambulistic torpor, not unlike the state of half-embalmed bodies which are not in the basement, though they might as well be.

Events continue conspiring.

At this point, as with all Fourth Seasons, interest begins to wane. Can the producers pull this off? Can our attention be recaptured? Now that the initial hook has lost its ... hook ... can we be ... rehooked? Can these separate strands be woven together into a cohesive whole? Like cloth? Or a winding sheet? Or will things simply unwind. Then rewind. Then unwind. *Ad infinitum*, like life.

But this isn't life, this is an HBO series. Unlike life, it has to have a narrative arc. However contrived or obscure. Otherwise what would be the point? Who would care? No one. Not even the fish.

But wait a minute, hold the phone. This isn't an actual series, this is a *pitch*, for crissakes. I can pause whenever. Like now.

* * *

A week ago my daughter started speaking to me. Actual sentences. Not only that, she turned off her iPod. Something was up. Turns out she wanted me to take her driving. Other than routinely hiding in the Jeep when she was seven and pretending she was driving to Mexico, she's never been behind the wheel.

"The first lesson in driving is to understand that the automobile is a powerful and deadly weapon," I said.

"You look pretty today, Mom," she said.

I was struck dumb. So much for the tough love approach. Maybe I should've gone for a more traditional method.

My father taught me to drive by taking me out on the back-roads behind the ore dumps, lighting up a La Palina, and telling me to go for it. I was fourteen. No doubt he was following the example of his father, who taught him to swim by throwing him off the end of a dock. He was three. My father went on to letter in swimming in high school, taking State in the butterfly. I went on to break a few neighborhood speed records, but never quite made it to the Wreck 'Em Rodeo over at the Speedway.

My husband objects to our daughter learning to drive. After all, she's barely fourteen. He has a point. But my husband grew up in civilized society. I grew up on the Iron Range.

Up on the Range we learned to drive young, and we learned to drive fast. When we finally acquired the Holy Grail, a driver's license, we spent every possible waking moment cruising the main drag in our parents' cars — First Avenue to Howard Street to 23rd and back again — over and over for hours and hours in a relentless mind-numbing circle, smalltown kids locked in a compulsion to recognize the make and model of every other circling car, and the silhouettes of the teenagers within. Until it finally occurred to us that maybe what we were searching for in all those other vehicles was not each other, but ourselves.

Nosireebob! That's not me in that Blue LeMans! Maybe I finally saw the light and got the fuck outta Dodge!

Eventually many of us did. Get the fuck outta Dodge. But not before acquiring lasting muscle memories from all that endless driving around and around through the same limited landscape like hellbent gerbils, wanting nothing so much as to escape.

And it was while gripped in the throes of this forgotten muscle memory that it came to me. As I headed out in search of the proper venue in which to introduce my daughter to the ancient art of operating a motor vehicle, I glanced over to where she sat panting with anticipation in the passenger seat, and I knew what I had to do.

"Hold onto your earbuds!" I instructed, and hung a hard left.

Which is how I came to spend last Saturday in the dying light of a gloomy November afternoon being driven endlessly around a graveyard, courtesy of my daughter, whose only vehicular experience up to that point had been driving me to drink. Around and around she circled, eyes wide, lips clamped shut, hands at ten and two, while I barked commands:

"Turn right at Jesus! Watch out for that angel! Pull over by the Garden of Precious Lambs!"

If you think about it, a cemetery is the perfect environment for the beginning driving experience. A quiet little ghost town of roadways and neighborhoods, nestled in a beautiful parklike setting, offering countless driving opportunities in a 5mph speed limit. And after you've cruised the place a few dozen times, the gravestones start to look like buildings — homes and offices, restaurants and markets, a storage unit! a gay bar! — and you begin to entertain the possibility of maybe even spotting a few local inhabitants. Your eyes narrow, you stare intently, until it finally occurs to you that maybe it's not one of them you're worried about seeing, but yourself.

Nosireebob! That's not me over by that fresh mound of dirt! Maybe I finally saw the light and got the fuck on the wagon!

Eventually it grew too dark to read the names on the markers, and my daughter and I switched seats and headed for home.

"The summer I was fifteen," I ruminated nostalgically, turning into our alley, "I finally got my permit, I could take Driver's Ed. And you know what? *I even remember the instructor's name.*"

"'That was like, a hundred years ago," said my daughter, staring into the darkness, lost in the afterglow of her first time.

"His name was Ed," I said, "Ed Simonich." I parked the car, turned off the ignition, waited.

"Ed," I said again into the darkness. "Think about it ..."

"Oh, I get it," said my daughter after a while. "Driver's Ed."

And for a nanosecond I saw it, she actually smiled.

* * *

I advised my daughter to run away. Was that a bad thing? I was just brainstorming. As usual, I was driving her to gym.

"I hate you and I hate this fucking family," she said from the passenger side of things.

So I offered up the above suggestion. I was on the High Bridge, following some asshole with a dead deer strapped to his penis.

What we have here, I said to myself, *is a dead deer.*

This child I'm raising — let's call her my daughter, for the sake of argument, which is what we do — wants to be somewhere else. Someone else. She changes her name at school, studies her face in the mirror, calls my bluff. Am I bluffing? I didn't used to think so.

Meanwhile, I look in the mirror and Shirley Booth stares back at me. Not the *Hazel* Shirley Booth, who'd fix things in a jiffy then scramble up a pie. The *Come Back, Little Sheba* Shirley Booth, who schlumps around in her housecoat all day mooning over her long lost dog.

What we have here, I said to myself, *is a lost dog.*

If my dog ever goes missing — and I wouldn't blame her — I'll be right behind.

When we first brought this dog home, my daughter was afraid of her. That was seven years ago. At the time, my daughter still looked at me with wonder. Now I know what she was wondering about.

But my daughter was afraid of the new puppy and avoided the floor for much of first grade. I envisioned a children's book, *The Girl Who Lived on the Back of the Couch*. It had possibilities, I thought, but like so much else, ended up on the slush pile.

Since then my daughter has come down from the furniture. Now we're all afraid of *her*.

It wasn't always this ... bad. It took a while. Eighth grade clinched the deal.

When I was in eighth grade, I knew my parents were utter morons, but I kept this knowledge to myself. My father's blood pressure was the reason. You don't push an ornery Finn who studied classical piano and studied to be a forest ranger but instead ended up in some remote suburb of Palookaville raising three daughters and selling front-end loaders to rednecks. You just *don't*.

My daughter would push me off the High Bridge if she could. But not before pocketing the car keys.

What we have here is a slush pile.

I have these memories of my daughter, snuggled up next to me at bedtime, surrounded by an island of stuffed animals, sloe eyes moving across the pages of a book as I read. Of course one book was never enough, and we kept a wobbly pile of extras on the rug beside the bed.

I don't recall when it first happened, but one night during this bedtime ritual, I started making up my own stories. I'd finish a book, take another from the pile, open it and begin reading:

Once upon a time there was a girl who lived on the back of the couch ...

This evolved into a sort of game: how far into a story could I get before my daughter called my bluff. Before she'd grin with delight, grab another book, ask me to do it again. And again. Eventually I'd insert something too outlandish into the narrative, even for a children's story (*... and then Little Franny Fox looked toward the pond and Elvis was walking across the water and his hair was perfect ...*), and that was our signal for calling it a night.

My daughter's mission in this ritual was to recognize which stories were real and which were made up. Her labels. And I let her have them. At the time, she was too young to understand that all stories are made up. Now we both know differently. We know all stories are real.

KANSAS, FAREWELL

I'm sitting by the fire with a book and a glass of wine last Saturday evening when my cell phone starts vibrating. It's my daughter, texting. From the TV room on the second floor.

Remember that movie from the old days about the babysitter who keeps getting scary phone calls? She finally calls the operator, who stays on the line to determine where the calls are coming from. The phone rings again, it's the scary caller, suddenly the operator's voice interrupts:

"Get out of the house now! He's calling from the upstairs extension!"

I've always been a sucker for a scary movie, a ghost story, or better yet, a *true* ghost story. Not so my daughter. What used to scare kids shitless back in the day gets no reaction from her, who isn't afraid of anything. Or so she'd have you believe.

My daughter rarely texts me, but she's desperate. My husband disabled all the usual contacts on her cell phone except for emergency numbers, i.e., her parents and the people down the block who call her to babysit. Why, you ask, did my husband do such a diabolical thing? Here's a hint: what does the word "fuck" start with? How about more than one fuck?

We're talking a multi-fuck report card.

Last month my daughter sent over 4,000 texts. She even sleeptexts, her thumbs twitching across the blankets like jumping beans. When I pick her and her teammates up from gymnastics, they text each other on the ride home in the car. I feel like I'm transporting a bunch of rhesus monkeys.

Speaking of which, a monkey could've gotten a better report card.

If I would've come home with such a report card when I was fourteen, I would've been dropped at the orphanage. First I would've been beaten, then dropped. But these days you can't get away with that. How they expect us to manage these hooligans is beyond me, but there will be no blood.

I think my daughter would've preferred a good beating to having her cell phone euthanized. In her world it's like pulling the plug on a beloved relative. Not that she beloves any of her relatives lately, certainly not Yours Truly. But, as I said, she must've been desperate, her thumbs couldn't control themselves.

"wat r u up 2?" she texts.

"I'm trying unsuccessfully to get shitfaced," I text back.

(Kidding!)

"I'm sitting beside the fire reading a rather slow-moving novel, gazing through the piano window at the gently falling snow," is what I wrote.

I try to give my daughter a subliminal literary experience whenever I text her, lest she start believing that "r" and "u" and "2" are the correct spellings. But I trust she'll figure that out when she's thirty and working on her GED.

When I was in eighth grade, we passed notes. Hand-written, on paper, with pens and pencils. A fruitful day might produce a half dozen, slipped surreptitiously into a friend's palm while passing in the hallways.

I actually have an old shoebox full of the things, which a friend saved and presented to me when *I* turned thirty. Maybe it was forty. I still occasionally look through them when I'm in the mood for a good bout of mortified cringing. You rarely see so many exclamation points anymore!!!!! And once I'd acquired an actual boyfriend, I began displaying the symptoms of full-blown mania. Instead of dotting my lower case "i"s in the traditional manner, I started drawing little circles atop them, and my handwriting took on a distinct backward slant. In one instance, I encircled a wrinkled spot in the margin, with an arrow pointing to this explanation: *Here is where a tear from my heart fell!!!!!*

I've told my daughter about the old days, when we used to pass notes in school. She rolls her eyes and asks if we had electricity back then. Once when we were at her grandparents' house down in The City, she pulled me aside into her father's childhood bedroom.

"What's this?" she said.

She wasn't a teenager yet, she still asked me things. She was pointing to a rotary telephone on the nightstand. My husband grew up in Edina, they had phones in the bedrooms.

"That's a phone, silly," I said.

"Yeah, right," she said.

Which was the same thing she said when I told her that Christians believe Jesus is the Son of God. She was in second grade at the time.

Now she's not. And we're not in Kansas anymore.

Meanwhile, back at the fireside, where snow is gently falling, I'm recalling the previous evening, when a friend stopped by for confessions and cocktails, we called it. We were sitting around another such fire, me regaling her with an endless list of ongoing woes, when a loud bang shook the house under our feet.

"And not only that," I said, with a nod at the floor, "we've got Morlocks in the basement!"

Actually it was our ancient furnace shuddering to life, but it took another cocktail to calm my guest down.

My daughter texts me again.

"yr txt made me lol," she writes. So much for subliminal literacy.

"Our texting reminds me of that movie," I write back, *"where the operator tells the babysitter the calls are coming from the upstairs phone."* It takes me a while to type this, the words scroll off the screen into outerspace, er, cyberspace.

When I first got a phone with a qwerty keyboard, I laid it out on a tabletop and carefully placed my fingers in the correct touch-type position. This was before I figured out thumb-typing. Or before I figured out why it's called qwerty. Do you know why it's called qwerty? Just texting, er, testing.

A log falls. I raise my glass, my phone vibrates again. This is maybe a dozen vibrations in as many minutes. I've already broken any and all standing note-passing records from the old days.

"wats a operator?" texts my daughter.

I drain my glass and pour another. I'm losing sensation in my thumbs.

"!!!!!!!!!!!!!" I text back.

I send that, then text again:

"Here is where a tear from my heart fell!!!!! –> ( )."

I don't hear from my daughter for a few minutes, and I start to wonder. Should I go check on her? Then my phone vibrates.

"sory fell asleep," she writes.

It is, after all, after midnight. I picture her beautiful eyes closing, her precious phone resting open on her heart.

Then she writes:

"btw y r u cryin???!!!"

After a few seconds, she writes again:

"goin 2 bed gnite."

I close my phone, look out at the snow. I wonder, is it midnight in Kansas? Are they in the same time zone? I make a mental note to google it, and turn back to my novel, which is moving as slow as ever.

* * *

The other evening at the eighth grade choir concert, I run into an old colleague. I haven't seen him in fifteen years. We chat for a bit, catch up. He's holding writing workshops at a local college, spending the summer in Spain, publishing his fourth book of poetry.

"And what are *you* up to?" he says.

I look around for the morphine drip.

"I teach preschool," I say.

Sometimes it's all you have left. The truth.

A former student of mine has named her pet after me. A fish. She's now six. The student, not the fish. If this fish lives to be six days, I'll eat my hat. Actually, I don't wear hats, I have a weird-shaped head. Sort of like a fish.

"This is new territory," I said to Former Student's mother, when she popped in to tell me about my latest namesake. Last year I had a Barbie named after me, which is more like it.

Maybe I should've mentioned the fish to Old Colleague. He, of all people, should understand irony.

The preschoolers pronounce "ironing" like "irony," with a hard *r*.

"I'm i-ron-ing my wedding dress," says Brittany, when I ask what she's doing with that roll of paper towel.

The paper towel is draped over the yellow plastic ironing board and trails across the carpet like a winding sheet. Later she and Benjamin, who've been playing house, decide they don't need a baby after all and put it back in the dryer.

Old Colleague appears to have taken something *out* of the dryer.

Old Colleague's maybe ten years older than I, if that's possible, and here he is, with a daughter in eighth grade. This is not the same daughter from fifteen years ago. Sneaking a glance, I determine it's not the same wife, either.

My daughter and I are in the car, headed for the local alternative high school, where we're due for a guided tour. I ask if she knows a girl named Anderson in the eighth grade, Anderson being Old Colleague's name.

"You're fucking joking," says my daughter.

I take this as a positive sign. She hasn't spoken to me in thirty-seven hours.

"She's probably blonde," I say, trying to hide my excitement, "with blue eyes."

My daughter stares at me, mouth agape. I notice — more excitement! — that her retainer's in! It didn't fall out of her pocket onto East Eighth Street after all!

The students — that is, the entire student body — of the middle school where my daughter has been doing time, were evacuated from the building on Monday while police dogs cased the joint. When this latest bomb threat was determined to be yet another in a long line of fake bomb threats, a cop allowed my daughter to pet one of them. The dogs, not the cops.

"He licked my hand," my daughter told me.

Those were her last words, until now.

"Do you know how many blonde-blue-eyed Andersons there are in that fucking craphole?" she says from the passenger seat, her retainer flashing in the sunlight streaming through the moonroof.

I consider mentioning that her graduating class at the alternative school will consist of less than fifty students, but think better of it. Instead, I reapply my sunglasses and turn Lady Gaga up to warp nine.

I'm absolutely mad about Lady Gaga. She positively sends me. My daughter wanted to send me to a Home when she found out about this. She'd asked me what I wanted for my birthday, and I told her a Lady Gaga CD.

"You're perverted," she said. Then she narrowed her eyes. "How do you even *know* about Lady Gaga?"

My daughter thinks I live in a cave when it comes to contemporary culture. Pretty much she's right.

But I do have my moments.

I was driving to work a while back when I turned on the radio, which just happened to be tuned to one of my daughter's favorite stations, where some bee-otch just happened to be shouting about not wanting to be friends, just wanting to fuck (sentiments, my husband likes to remind me, I expressed to *him* the first time we met, in no uncertain terms), and ooh-la-la, sis-boom-bah, that was it. My hair stood on end. My palms started to itch. I almost rear-ended a Miller Lite truck.

You know it when you hear it. The real thing. I wanted to lace up the ol' Oberhamers and hit the pavement.

Once a month my daughter's school receives a bomb threat. When I was her age, Patty Tucker got suspended for demonstrating the twist during after-school enrichment. Next thing you know, Kennedy was shot.

I was in math class when the news about the President came over the PA. Mr. Johnson started crying. Not the Vice President, the math teacher. A man who fried students for breakfast alongside his Jimmy Deans. After the announcement the silence in the hallways was palpable. We shut our lockers and wandered home like the living dead, into that long surreal weekend in front of the Motorolas. All those black-and-white images etched forever onto the rest of our lives — the horse with the backward boots, the long black veil, John-John's salute, the drums.

I once knew a girl who'd been in a car accident when she was a teenager, in which another girl was killed. The first girl saw her life in two parts: before the accident, and after. An entire generation experienced this same split: there was life before Dallas, and life after. The afterlife.

The monthly bomb threats are fallout from the afterlife.

The first time I picked up the phone and heard some male voice telling me there was *a situation at the school,* I felt my heart stop. Now I hang up before the message finishes. Same old, same old, where'd I leave my coffee.

After the first few times, when she looked at me like she might be talking to an escapee, I stopped mentioning the bomb threats to my daughter. I later found out a couple of the threats had been written on the wall in the girls' can, in lipstick. The students are always locked down for a period of time in their classrooms, during which they can text-message each other and, as a special treat, are allowed to chew gum.

My daughter started kindergarten on September 12, 2001. Another brilliant blue day — like the day before — minus the drone of the daily 7:36 descending ontime toward the airport. We live in the kind of town where one looks up when one hears a plane, which are rare. As we waited under the silent blue sky beside the big red tree for the bright orange bus, my daughter was unaware of the events of the previous day. 9/11. Her generation's Dallas.

But my daughter had already had her own personal Dallas, five years and eight months earlier. Call it an accident of birth.

When my daughter came accidentally into the world, I was in another state. Not the state of bliss following the cessation of labor, or the state of denial, or the state of Texas. I was halfway across the country in a place where America blends into Canada blends into the wild. The borderland. Between what had been, and what would be. Where I was waiting. For the other shoe. And the bomb. And the aftermath. And the life after that.

Old Colleague and I are commiserating about the sorry state of affairs at the middle school.

"If it's Monday, there must be a bomb threat," I say.

"How many is this now?" he says.

"Nine," I say, "maybe forty."

I'm trying to recover from my unfortunate career revelation. If I can prove an intact wit, I might still stand a chance. Maybe he'll think I was just pulling his leg about the preschool thing.

Just then my husband gets a text message. Did I mention my husband is here? He reads it, texts back, reaches for his jacket.

"Somebody's hungry," he says, "time to hit the road."

"Our daughter prefers not to be seen in public with us," I say, wittily, to Old Colleague. "She communicates by code."

"They're all the same, aren't they?" says Old Colleague, smiling, shaking his successful old head, and I'm thinking, No, no they're not all the same, not by a long shot, jack.

I leave, then, before Old Colleague's daughter materializes. I just don't want to know, don't want to be reminded. Of everything, of nothing. My husband follows me through the crowd, down the main hallway, out past the entrance doors, to where our daughter is waiting at the top of the steps, brown eyes watching, iPod in place.

"What's for dinner?" she asks, too loudly, over music only she can hear.

We walk down the stairs, out onto East Eighth Street. I look over at my husband.

"There's pasta from last night," he says.

"Refried beans from Tuesday," I say.

I look back at our daughter, who shrugs and looks away and turns the music up.

I go outside to escape the words, the words, the dog jumps at the door to follow. Later in bed beside me she is sobbing. In her sleep, a sound I've never heard. My heart breaks not for the last time. The last time something was lost and not found. Too many times. Too many glasses of wine.

Sober people are all alike; every drunkard is a drunkard in her own way.

When I look out the side window the apple tree is in bloom. Why didn't I know this? Too busy putting a year away, wrapping things up, saying goodbye. Leavetaking. Out on the playground, that last day, the preschoolers cawed wildly, their faces upturned. And I wanted to teach them one last thing, I wanted to teach them murder.

A group of crows, *I wanted to say,* is called a murder, isn't that strange?

But these children wouldn't have known that word. To live in a world where some words don't.

And I'll always wonder. If she wanted to teach you one last thing, if she wanted to tell you about your father. Did she teach you that word? Did she say it was him? Before you were gone, did she want you to know? But how could you not, you were there, in that car, and out on the street the unthinkable.

So, you see, it wasn't the lunch box. Or the jacket. Not even the iPod. That next lost thing in a lifetime of things lost. It was the murder of childhood out on the playground, children's faces drinking the sky. Once upon a time you should have been among them. Instead I imagine you outside the fence, on your chubby toddler legs, watching the scene like Disney, knowing all the words by heart. While deep in your ears there lived other words, other sounds. Do they live there still?

You are my heart, *I tell you,* that's where you live.

It's dark now. The words have retreated to their shadowy corners. Tomorrow I will find the bee, engorged and enormous in the basement, bumping against the window toward the light. And I'll do what I always do, that thing with a glass and a postcard. And the bee will do what bees always do, when I release them out into the world again: turn around and head straight at me, buzzing murderously, as if I were to blame.

SHRAPNEL

Here's how you get your fourteen-year-old daughter to go to the Loony Bin: you lie. It isn't really a Loony Bin, it's a Residential Treatment Center. In the old days we called it the Loony Bin.

Here's what you *don't* say:

"We're at our wits' end, you've completely lost your marbles, you're going to the Loony Bin."

Here's what you *do* say:

"Take a shower, wear clean underwear, we're going for a drive."

If the fourteen-year-old in question is at least one point above plant life, she'll no doubt ask the following:

"Where are we driving *to?*"

You're prepared for this. Resist the temptation to admonish her about ending a sentence with a preposition. Instead, say:

"We're going to meet a new therapist."

That's what they're called these days, therapists. In the old days we called them the guys in the white coats.

As you drive to the Loony Bin to see the guys in the white coats, turn to the fourteen-year-old in the backseat and say:

"What a beautiful day!"

She'll never suspect a thing, you're always saying inane bullshit like this. Because if you said:

"How are you *feeling* about this?"

she'd immediately become suspicious and jump from the moving vehicle. The reason for all this subterfuge is to prevent just such an occurrence.

For instance, if you'd sat her down the previous evening and attempted to explain this upcoming event, no matter how you presented it, she would've reacted negatively. In the old days we called this going bonkers. As in, first she'd go bonkers, then she'd run the fuck away.

After meandering through the countryside for a while, when you finally pull up in front of the Loony Bin, don't say:

"It's not as bad as juvy, but it ain't no summer camp."

Instead, say:

"What a beautiful campus!"

As Loony Bins go, it *is* a lovely setting. Two hundred acres of woods and meadows, old growth pine, a gymnasium, animal barns. Of course none of this matters, because the truth is, you've just lured an unsuspecting fourteen-year-old here under false pretenses. In the old days we called this pulling a fast one.

At this point, here's what you say to *yourself*:

"Fuckenay, I just pulled a fast one."

By the time the guys in the white coats have explained to your daughter that she'll be staying at the Loony Bin for a while, that she'll be their special guest, you're all so hopelessly lost in the labyrinth of the grand old building, you couldn't find your way out again to save your sorry ass souls.

Resist the temptation to say:

"Did anybody keep track of the number of locked doors we just passed through?"

Instead, say:

"This is the safest place on earth."

At this point, if you have an ounce of cajones left, you ask everyone else to leave, to please wait out in the hallway, and they do (first they unlock the door). Then you turn to your daughter and say:

"Do you trust me?"

By now she'll be glaring daggers at you (in the old days we called it giving you the evil eye). Ignore this, and say it again:

"*Do you trust me?*"

She has no choice. You've finally gotten her attention. There's nothing to be done. She nods.

Here's where you say:

"Everything is going to be okay."

Then you say it again. Whether or not you believe it.

Now there's nothing left to do but leave. You follow the guys in the white coats back through the locked doors (there are five), out into the shrieking sun, to the parking lot.

Here's where you look back, once. Then you get in your car, turn the key, and begin the long road home.

* * *

Ten years ago July 5th our daughter arrived. We called her our little firecracker. Turns out she was more like a grenade. She finally pulled the pin.

Or maybe the pin was set on a ten-year delay, and she pulled it the moment she stepped off that plane in her yellow organdy "wedding dress." I saved the dress, along with the black patent leather Mary Janes I bought her, like other mothers save baptismal gowns and worn out baby shoes.

Recently I heard from a friend who wrote to tell me that her brother died, followed two weeks later by her cat, and I catapulted back in time to this: in the space of twenty months, my mother died, my father died, my cat died, my dog died.

Just like that.

Between my mother and my father — that is, between their deaths — our daughter arrived in her yellow dress. She called it her wedding dress because, she told us, she'd worn it to a wedding, and the bride told her she was pretty. The wedding was in California, as was she, in her fourth? fifth? foster family, I forget.

But she wasn't in California any longer, we told her, now she was "home."

Whatever that means.

When our daughter fell from the sky into our lives, the first order of business was to calm her terror at meeting the husky. We later learned she'd been mauled by a dog in the second? third? foster family, I forget. The next order of business was to rid her four-and-a-half-year-old head of generations of head lice. We must've been napalming great-great-great-grandparents in that bathtub, *yessireebob*.

I can still see her stretched out on the porcelain, brown hair streaming toward the drain, brown eyes squinting steadily at the ceiling light, a stoic if slightly undersized buddha. We later learned delousing was a routine experience for her, right up there with teeth-brushing and bed-wetting.

But for the dog and the cat, the entire household acquired lice, including the people, the rugs, the clothes, the linen, half of the furniture, and one of the neighbors. At the time, we told ourselves this was symbolism at its best, the ultimate literary device at work. Washing away the old life, welcoming in the new.

Except the old life has proved resistant to the last, a dark horse stalking us like a shadow, tenacious and inevitable.

"After the first death, there is no other."
When my mother died, I believed I finally understood what the poet meant. Cats, dogs, babies, dreams ... somehow I survived all the losses. And then my mother died, and the world changed in a nanosecond. Utterly. Forever.

Just like that.

Never again, I thought, it will never happen like that again.

But. Now. This. Death of a different kind. A child (*not mine, mine, not mine*) in danger of herself. And the world has changed one more time.

The first order of business in this new world is learning how to move around in it, how not to come in contact with anything. It's the shrapnel. I didn't think grenades contained shrapnel, I was wrong. It's everywhere. The people, the rugs, the clothes, the linen, half of the furniture, and one of the neighbors. The entire household has acquired shrapnel, including the dog and the cat.

I've got a piece lodged an inch from my heart, if you can believe that. And I'm afraid to sit down due to a couple of good-sized chunks in my ass. I was able to remove the shard by my left eye, but a tear duct was damaged in the process, and I can't stop weeping.

I want to lay our daughter down in the bathtub and napalm this all away. Out with the old, etc. Trouble is, she no longer fits. Not stretched out in the bathtub, for starters, and she's rapidly outgrowing other venues as well. Drugs won't help. That's what Dr. Else says, can you believe that? A shrink named Dr. Else.

"You can't medicate this away," says Dr. Else. "You can't love it away."

Thanks for telling me, doc. Anything *else* I should know?

I find myself doing insomniac drunken 2 a.m. googling. *Borderline Personality, Attachment Disorder, Adjustment Disorder, PTSD.* Followed by a three-hour session of Free Cell in yet another in a continuing series of useless attempts to clear my blown-out brain.

Last night while I was (miraculously!) sleeping, two explosions occurred. *In my dreams!* There I am, morphing along through yet another in a continuing series of useless dream-scenes, when *KA-BAM!* there's an explosion just offstage. A couple scenes later, it happens again, right beside me, *KA-BAM!* I wake up and check the sheets for blood.

Beginning just after her first birthday, our daughter lived with us for half a year. But she arrived with strings attached. Big complicated knotted-up strings. In the form of a big complicated knotted-up birth mother. A niece, to be exact.

At the time, we lived outside of town, in the woods beside the river. While the niece/birth mother watched soap operas and blew smoke up the chimney and speed-dialed California from the sofa bed down in the rec room, I'd wander the woods beside the river with the baby, pointing out various woodsy, rivery things: *grosbeak! dragonfly! red pine! woodtick!*

If the weather didn't cooperate — and this is some of the most uncooperative weather on the planet, jack — the baby and I would hang out in the house in the first floor great room, wandering an ever-shifting landscape of baby toys. She loved the dolls and the blocks and the books and the stuffed animals, but her favorite by far was a plastic musical toy which sat on the floor and played several familiar children's songs. *Twinkle*

Little Star, Playmate, Mary Had a Little Lamb, Pop Goes the Weasel. She'd push one song after another after another and sway in a wobbly circle on her chubby legs, flashing a killer dimple and squinting her eyes in delight.

When our daughter left us — that is, when we put the niece / birth mother / baby on a plane back to California — we stuffed as many items as we could into their shabby suitcases, including the plastic musical toy. Three years later, when our now four-and-a-half-year-old-soon-to-be-adopted daughter returned alone in that yellow dress, she brought the musical toy with her, tucked deep at the bottom of her suitcase.

By this time we'd moved into our current house in town. We placed the toy in the bump out — the California room, we call it, filled as it is with plants and sun, with a view of the back-yard — on a low shelf beside the patio door, and there it has stayed. Through the years one or another of us has occasionally taken it out and reenacted the song and dance routine from that time on the river, in that way families have of ritualizing certain memories.

Then late on the afternoon of June 4th, six weeks ago, our daughter stood at the kitchen counter on her sturdy gymnast's legs and ate a bottle of ibuprofen.

Sometime in the early hours of June 5th, as my husband and I drank wine in the California room and stared out at the darkness while our pumped-out drugged-up daughter crashed in the room above us, the musical toy began, by itself, to play.

Just like that.

Was it the heat? the humidity? the shrapnel? What I know is this: the toy proceeded to play, briefly and sporadically, from its perch on the shelf by the door, for several weeks. Symbolism at its best, the ultimate literary device at work. Until finally, unable to bear such pathos any longer, my husband turned it over, and it stopped.

* * *

After my daughter ate a few dozen ibuprofen in an effort to change the game, I started moving the pig around. Under the bird feeder, next to the red pine, over by the swing set.

This is not an easy pig. My husband thinks 75-80 pounds. I bought her with the help of a Gift Card the preschoolers gave me on the last day of school. The next day my husband and I drove in the hot noon sun to a garden center on the outskirts of town, looking for petunias. I found one, only not the kind that grows in a pot. I turned a corner and there she stood, sun rays shooting out around her like a halo.

After we'd hauled her home (rather, after my husband hauled her home) and corralled her in her first location beneath the bird feeder, I started thinking about a name.

Not for a moment did I consider Petunia. Or even Wilbur. Take me out and shoot me if I'm ever typical. By the time the moon rose that evening in a night shot with stars, I'd decided on the perfect moniker for this new and unusual piece of statuary: Charlotte. So I named a pig after a spider, so what. Stranger things have happened.

And then, one of them did.

When someone you think you know, to say nothing of love, does something so completely out of left field as to stand at the kitchen counter and eat thirty ibuprofen, the first thing you realize is this: you really don't know this person. The second thing is this: you are now in a whole new ball game. Suddenly there you are, new game, new rules, you're playing with a stranger, you don't know the score.

And there it is, the truth: you don't know the score. Even though you used to. Even if most of the time you were fucking behind, even if you were fucking losing, you knew the fucking score. Not only that, you knew your position. You knew where you should be and what was expected of you. You knew what your job was. You were expected to play, to the best of your ability, the game.

Now someone has gone and changed the game. There are other truths, but this is the truth you have come to.

When my husband and I went to the South of France two years ago, I brought back a pig. A flying pig. A cast iron flying pig who weighs as much as a small lawnmower, with wings outstretched and an upturned cherubic face.

The customs officials called her *le cochon d'ange*, the Angel Pig, and she created quite a stir going through security. Improbable as she was, I carried her with me in the taxis and through the airports and on the planes, and I knew from the beginning exactly where her place would be, once we got home: on the sideboard in the bump out beside the white ginger jar lamp.

Not so with Charlotte. Charlotte's a pig of a different color.

To begin with, Charlotte is nowhere near cherubic. Her expression is far from blissful. Truth be told, Charlotte looks like she'd as soon bite you as look at you. Though it's anyone's guess why, Charlotte is one royally pissed-off pig. Which is in part why I fell for her. Her crabby substantiality charmed me.

The fact is, pissed-off or not, Charlotte weighs as much as a small piano, and keeping my husband's back in mind, I immediately installed her beneath the bird feeder with the intention of its being a permanent placement. Then my daughter went and had her little snack, and ever since, for reasons unknown, Charlotte's been on the roam.

I know she belongs somewhere, I just don't know where. I go back and forth, visualizing scenarios, but she's become almost impossible to place. One minute she's ensconced mid-lawn amongst the hawkweed, the next, she guards the birdbath while the starlings shower her with indifference.

Sometimes I imagine that when she finally finds her true home, her expression will change. She'll gradually begin to relax, maybe even break a smile. Here I am, expecting something miraculous, and I'm not even a believer.

Although I do believe in some things. That life can change on a dime. That a ref can throw everyone out of the game and call it a day and leave town. That there's nothing you can fucking do about it. That if you continually move a 75-pound concrete pig around your backyard, you're going to pay for it. Or rather, your husband will.

And it's just his luck, there's not an ibuprofen to be found.

TO SAY NOTHING OF WOLVES

There's a toilet seat in the window of our garage. You can see it from the alley as you drive past. It's been there all summer, I only just discovered this. Like I'm the last to know.

My husband put it there, who else. He claims it was the only shelf space left. When I complained, aghast, he told me to put up curtains. In the garage? Only people from New Jersey do that.

My husband has absolutely no sense of feng shui. He calls it "fun shit."

"All that fun shit," he says, "that's your job. My job is to pay for everything."

He's got a point.

But a toilet seat? In full view? What will the neighbors think? Nothing they haven't already. Still, it's hard enough being the resident bohos without such blatant advertising.

I noticed the toilet seat last weekend when I was driving back from the Funny Farm with my daughter. We used to say Loony Bin, now we say Funny Farm. I'd taken the long way home down the alley. Actually, my daughter saw it first.

"Mom," she said, "there's a toilet seat in the garage window."

"Good Christ," I said, sideswiping the neighbor's Virgin Mary statue.

I'm not sure if this was due to the toilet seat, or the fact that my daughter was talking to me. I'm trying to get used to it, it's a habit she's picked up since her stay at The Farm.

My daughter was having her first overnight at home in more than two months. I tried to remember what it had felt like to return home from college for the first time. I remember thinking the house seemed really small.

"Mom," said my daughter, "the house seems really small."

I also remember feeling dizzy, like I might be dreaming, everything felt surreal.

"Mom," said my daughter, "I feel dizzy, like I'm dreaming, everything feels surreal."

Thirty-thousand in insurance to unearth a word like "surreal?"

After a shining performance in elementary school, our daughter flunked eighth grade. She stopped eating, stopped speaking to us, started staying away from the house. She took to stealing anything, anytime, anywhere, from anyone. She started drinking. Smoking weed. Throwing up. Cutting herself.

"Surreal" felt like a win.

During the next twenty-three hours and forty-eight minutes, my daughter ate and ate and ate, then slept for eleven hours and seventeen minutes, then rose again and ate some more. In between all this eating and sleeping she talked. And talked and talked and talked. And cried. And laughed. And talked some more. This from a child whose record for not speaking once stood at two months and ten days. The poor thing was in danger of hyperventilating from over-oratization. I was developing a mild case of tinnitus.

Three months ago the choice was clear: either let our daughter live in the TV room and leave trays of food outside the door until she was old enough to vote, or call The Farm. We opted for Door Number Two.

When I finally put my daughter back in the car last Saturday afternoon (with a bag of Lay's Pickle Chips and a bottle of Smartwater) and waved good-bye as my husband drove her away, I found myself wondering what it would take to keep her at The Farm until, say, the cows came home — or the llamas or the sheep or the pygmy goats, to name a few of the other residents.

Something was nagging at me, something ... surreal.

A few months earlier, at the intake interview, the psychologist had tried to prepare my husband and me for what lay ahead. The average stay at The Farm for an adolescent with issues similar to our daughter's, he told us, was somewhere in the range of a year to eighteen months. And yet here she was, after so short a time, responding so well. Or so it seemed.

But this thought was just a momentary lapse, like so many other momentary lapses. Like, for instance, when one lapses momentarily and lobs a broken toilet seat onto a stack of old shingles, not considering that there just might possibly be another point of view. Like the one from the alley, for instance.

I glanced over my shoulder, hoping against hope, but it was still there, glowing like the moon in the garage window. The choice was clear. Either roll up my sleeves and start reorganizing — which could take until people stopped making jokes about New Jersey — or measure for curtains.

I stepped into the garage and looked around. Even if I opted for Plan B, I couldn't get anywhere near the window until I'd reorganized everything else. I eyed the overflowing recycling bin. The wall of seventies sound equipment. The maze of trash cans and live traps and gardening paraphernalia and dead two-stroke engines.

I felt dizzy, like I was dreaming, everything felt surreal.

"*Let the fun shit begin,*" I said to myself, and rolled up my sleeves.

* * *

So the kid's at the Funny Farm, only nobody's laughing.

Except the preschoolers. They laugh all day. They think everything's funny. These days I'm taking my cue from them.

Take, for instance, Wednesday. Not the day, the word. *Wednesday.* The preschoolers think it's hilarious. They say it over and over until it comes out all wonky, by which time they're rolling on the floor like cue balls, laughing their little round heads off. Then there's *February.* They can't get past the first syllable without spitting up all over the big ABC rug in an effort to hold back hysteria.

And that's just *words.* Can you imagine what mayhem ensues when the teacher can't find her glasses ... *again?* or the phone rings during Silent Time? or one of them accidentally farts? I thought I'd have to break out the EpiPen the time Kara emerged from the bathroom trailing a banner of toilet paper from her teddy bear leggings.

This year we have a non-English-speaking student in class, and the possibilities for hilarity are endless. I mean, the little monsters are just about ready for prime time. A typical exchange:

"Class," I say, "can you think of some words that start with the letter *T*?"

"Tent!" hollers Donald.

"Truck!" hollers Leon.

"Tinkerbell!" hollers Abigail.

130

"Ironman!" hollers Alejandro.

When the delirium subsides, having reminded myself once again that I'm actually getting paid to do this, I try a different tack.

"Class," I say, "how many fingers am I holding up?"

"Five!" hollers Deborah.

"Three!" hollers Martin.

"Eleven!" hollers Katherine.

"Ironman!" hollers Alejandro.

The preschoolers are big on hollering. Apparently Ironman is big in the Philippines.

My father was big on hollering, although not so big on the Philippines, where he was stationed during World War II. I think of him whenever Alejandro talks about "da Pillipeens."

My father having been a world class hollerer, I vowed never to become a hollerer myself. A promise I more or less managed to keep, with a few notable exceptions: hunters, snowmobilers, ex-husbands, and all those responsible for putting *Eat, Pray, Love* on the best-seller lists, you know who you are.

Then I became a parent.

Happy families are all alike, that's for sure. They all shop at Gap.

Being of the *unhappy* family variety, we've always shopped at Target.

So a few months back, during an offgrounds, the warden calls it, I took the kid to Target in a sentimental moment, and she broke down. In shampoo. I mean, she *went down*. Hit the floor. Seems the sheer number of choices was too much for her. I'm with her there, I've been known to start blathering aloud in lightbulbs.

So that's where I found her, on her knees one aisle over,

tears hidden behind a cascade of hair. I knelt down, took the bottles from her basket, pretended to read the labels.

"*'For Big Hair,'*" I read. "*'For Humongous Hair.'*"

"Mom," she whispered, "where were you? I didn't know where you were."

"*'For Morbidly Obese Hair,'*" I continued. "*'For Hair in Need of a Stomach Bypass.'*"

"*Mo-ommm!*" she whispered, and then she couldn't help it, she started to smile. Then she started to giggle. Then I started to giggle. Then we started to hiccup and snort and somehow managed to get to our feet and stagger through the store and out the automatic doors into the parking lot, where we leaned against each other and laughed until we cried, then cried some more.

That was October.

So now it's February. The kid's home for good. This ain't no offgrounds, it's three weeks today. So I stopped by Target and picked up a couple bottles of that shampoo, which I've gift-wrapped and plan to give to her on Monday, which is Valentine's Day. I'm hoping for a smile, but I'll settle for an eye roll. We're back to that.

I'm taking my cue from the preschoolers, for whom not all things humorous are equal. Because while they laugh at pretty much anything, the preschoolers believe the cupid silhouette I hung on the door is pretty much the funniest thing they've *ever ever ever* seen, and they might be onto something. Last year's class felt the same way. And the year before that.

* * *

The cat's dying and I'm driving home from work. I only just arrived at work, but I'm driving home because I forgot my glasses. I'm listening to a program about early onset dementia. Some expert is discussing the difference between normal forgetfulness due to aging, versus forgetfulness due to dementia.

"For example," says the expert, "you forget where you've put your glasses. You search high and low, and then find them sitting on top of your head. That's normal."

Do I know this guy? Is he normal? Did he interview me for this program?

When I get home, I find my glasses. Not on top of my head, in the freezer.

The cat's dying and the earth moves under Washington. Irene tears up the East Coast. The New York subway system shuts down.

"God's mad at the government!" says Michelle Bachmann. "Vote for me!"

My cousin is killed in a car accident. He's twenty-two years old and he's driving a Beemer.

"Sometimes God just needs another angel," says his family, whose vehicles all sport Bachmann bumper stickers, and I say,

"He's God, for crissakes! Why doesn't he fucking make another angel!"

"Don't vote for God!" I say.

The cat's dying and I find myself under the kitchen table at 3 a.m. During a thunderstorm. With the dog. Usually I find myself under the kitchen table at 3 a.m. for other reasons, not necessarily involving the dog.

I look around as a crash of lightning spotlights the room and notice a small dark shape beneath a nearby chair. Not the cat, my glasses. Meanwhile, the dog is sitting on top of my head.

If my husband had to choose between me and the dog, he'd be hard-pressed.

"We're hard-pressed!" says Michelle Bachmann. "Let's drill for oil in the Everglades!"

The cat's dying and I'm seeing a shrink. I started seeing the shrink before she started dying. The cat, not the shrink. There's a hummingbird at the feeder. The wind is out of the west and the daylilies are still blooming. The hops have reached the top of the arbor, a pair of fawns are asleep under the mugo pines.

I keep seeing the shrink, but so far I'm still the same size.

Unlike the cat, who keeps getting smaller and smaller. Soon she'll disappear altogether.

* * *

We have a little money saved and my husband proposed doing some work on the kitchen.

"Fuck the kitchen," I said, "I want a facelift."

"But the kitchen would benefit both of us," said my husband, "it's only fair," and I said,

"Like you wouldn't benefit from my getting a facelift?" and he admitted I had a point.

Just then the phone rang. Not the cobweb-festooned contraption on the wall, the one in my husband's pants.

"Who is it?" I mouthed.

"The kid," my husband mouthed back, "she says she's lost in the woods."

"But I just opened a beer!" I said aloud.

"Who was that?" said our daughter from the woods.

"It was Mom," said my husband, "she says 'I'll be right there!'"

"Tell her to bring my green Columbia," said our daughter. "Oh and my lavender brush. Oh and my other earphones. Oh and my allowance for a month."

Our daughter had set out in the general direction of the 7-

Eleven on her way to meet a friend, when she took a shortcut through the cemetery, which went so well that, in a stunning reenactment of "Little Red Riding Hood," she took a shortcut through the woods, except that her basket of goodies consisted of an iPod and a cell phone, and she wasn't on her way to visit Grandma but to rendezvous with an ex-roommate from the Funny Farm, to say nothing of wolves.

I can feel my face heading south even as I relate this story.

"Little Red Riding Hood" being the quintessential cautionary tale, I asked my brave little daughter afterward what she'd learned from her misadventure, and she said,

"To always keep my phone charged. The signal was down to one bar!"

To which I say, one bar is as good as the next.

As part of my battle plan to lift my facial muscles, to say nothing of my spirits (not to be confused with those other spirits I routinely lift), I recently visited the local cosmetic bar, er, counter in search of the latest snake oil. I'd last made this particular hegira sometime during the Clinton administration. Things had changed.

Ghostly wisps of scent rose from an aromatherapy diffuser at my elbow, new age music pumped from some mysterious unseen source. I half-expected a hookah to be lying about and damned if I wouldn't've had a hit. When a clerk eventually materialized from behind a glass shelving unit, I gasped. Not only was this clerk wearing a white lab coat (the guys in the white coats!), he was a he! It said so right there, on his name badge.

"How may I be of assistance?" chirped Tyler, my Customer Service Representative.

"Errr ... " I stammered, momentarily at a loss, when what I *really* wanted to say was:

"Bite me! You must be fucking joking! You were just learning to walk in your last lifetime when I started buying Yardley of London in this one!"

It's bad enough having to show my face in public these days, let alone at a place where it's in the job description of some post adolescent male to scrutinize it.

Oblivious to my angst, Tyler scrutinized, then putzed among the items on the glass shelving unit, then spun around and brushed my cheek with some product whose name sounded like the latest Ben and Jerry's flavor.

"This is *my* personal favorite," he twittered, while I tried my best to keep from mouthing "Who gives a fuck?", at which point I noticed the foundation he had on was blended rather nicely, although for my tastes he'd gone a little heavy on the blush.

Having finally made my desperate purchase, I couldn't get out of there fast enough. I was just beginning to recover a sense of dignity, to say nothing of balance, when I exited the mall and was hit by a 50-mph wind gust. The desperate purchase flew from my hand, and as I stumbled after it through a wall of pelting sleet, some elderly Marlboro man blowing smoke rings at the bus kiosk winked at me. Either that or he was experiencing a TIA.

I didn't stop to find out. Grabbing the desperate purchase from midair, I staggered to my car and drove away into the heart of a category five blizzard, which took me by surprise, but it shouldn't have. This is only mid-April, after all, we still have two months of winter left.

By the time I reached home, I was in whiteout conditions. Not to be confused with blackout, which is *my* personal favorite. I found the garage by ramming into it, likewise the back gate. There I took a deep breath and, putting one foot in front of the other (another time-honored battle plan), set out blindly and bravely in the general direction of the house. But for the frozen birdbath I rammed into in my search for the door, I might've been lost in the woods.

NOT IN A BRITISH ACCENT

Now I know why the Pilgrims left England. Forget religious freedom. It was the BLOODY RAIN.

We just returned from a trip to the British Isles, and it rained every single bloody day. For a bloody fortnight.

My first clue should've been on the flight over, when I peeled my eyelids open after seven hours in the air and a four-teen-minute nap and looked down from the window of the plane at a solid white mass stretching to the horizon on every side.

"Hon, look!" I croaked to my husband. "It's Iceland! Maybe Greenland!"

It was neither. It was the bloody Jet Stream, wrapped like a bloody straitjacket around the entire UK. Even the Bloody Queen had lost all authority. As far as I know it's still there. Check with the IOC.

My next clue should've been when we finally landed and were taxiing toward the terminal, where an enormous piece of construction loomed in the mist. I rubbed the condensation from my window to get a better look. An ark.

Actually I should've known from the outset this trip would be one for the record books.

A week prior to our departure — back home in The Colonies — it rained for forty days and forty nights. In one twenty-four-hour period. Creeks became rivers, rivers became waterfalls, The Big Lake flowed red (the bloody lake!), streets buckled and sank toward China, taking a few Ford Fiestas with them. It was downright biblical, I expected a plague of locusts at any moment. They're calling it a 500-year "weather event." Up until the last minute we didn't know whether we'd be flying to Europe or booking passage on an oar boat, possibly a submarine.

We finally got the all-clear, and our gondola (it was complimentary!) dropped us at the airport, where my husband attempted to board an international flight carrying a Swiss army knife. In his man purse. He claimed innocence, and they believed him. Bollocks! I think the man purse was the deciding factor. If it had been Yours Truly found with a knife in her shoulder bag, rest assured I'd be writing this from the Tower of London.

Forget that notorious Ruinator of international travel, Jet Lag. If ever again I have occasion to visit the UK, I'm going to first check on the whereabouts of her bitter and twisted first cousin, Jet Stream. What a skank. Make that bloody skank.

In a pub in Edinburgh we sampled an ale with that description. Not bloody skank. Bitter and twisted.

"Hon, it's your namesake!" croaked my husband and swilled another pint. Make that seven.

There we were, sampling and swilling our way across the Island, while Mother Nature gnashed at our heels like a hunting hound, with no regard for etiquette or protocol or bloody good manners, of which the Brits are the world's foremost authorities.

I mean, one might expect Mother Nature to make an appearance at Stonehenge, one might even welcome it. Ambience and all that bloody rot. And believe me, Ms. Nature didn't disappoint, whipping up a monsoon of bitter wind and twisted rain for our viewing pleasure. I survived no less than five bumbershoot reversals during a soggy attempt to commune with any wayward 5000-year-old Druidic spirits who might be gadding about.

But the only spirits to be found were in the mini-bar back at the hotel, and the only thing communicable was a bone-chilling ague that didn't let up until I saw my shadow again, Puxatawny Phil be gobsmacked. This shadow-sighting didn't occur until I'd set foot on *terra firma* again (as opposed to *terra soaka*) back home in The Colonies just south of the North Pole, where — nine-month winters and 500-year weather events notwithstanding — things had dried up rather nicely (which is more than I can say for Yours Truly). Apparently the sun has a sense of humor.

Not so Mother Nature. Mother Nature is one cheesed off wanker. Make that bloody cheesed off.

Not only did the rain follow us to Stonehenge, it followed us to Bath (even Ms. Nature occasionally gets the joke), then Birmingham, then London, where it shadowed us around Hyde Park and Buckingham Palace and Trafalgar Square, and lurked outside the National Gallery and the British Museum, before following us to that little pub in Soho where we dripped into our Guinnesses and tried in vain to get it to sod off.

Eventually we threw in the towels and wet-legged it up the coast to Scotland, where we toured Edinburgh and environs, bumbershoots in hand, and draped our classic 18th century room at the four-star George Hotel with our soggy knickers, before repairing to yet another local pub where shots of Speyside Single Malt and the aforementioned bitter and twisted did their best to assuage our knackered, waterlogged souls.

Now I know where the phrase "Keep Calm and Carry On" comes from. Forget Churchill and World War II. It's the official logo of the British Meteorological Office. And you know how the Brits always say "Keep a stiff upper lip?" It's so the rain won't nick down one's bloody throat and bloody drown one.

As the plane climbed toward cruising altitude on its way back to The Colonies, I drowned my sorrows (those that were left, most of them had *already* drowned) in my ninth glass of wine (it was complimentary!) and leaned my soggy head against my husband's soggy shoulder. We'd had to stand on the tarmac at Charles de Gaulle for forty-five minutes waiting to board. Needless to say it was raining. Even the bloody French had lost all authority.

"Hon," I croaked, "what's the first thing you're gonna do when we get home?"

"Sleep," yawned my husband. "You?"

"Eat, sleep, Target," I said.

"What're you gonna get?" said my husband.

"A bum ... brella," I said. "I left mine in Paris."

"Better that than your heart," said my husband. "That reminds me ... will you pick me up a Swiss army knife?"

"Bloody hell!" I said, and we raised our plastic glasses in a toast.

Just then the plane shuddered violently. I looked out. It appeared we'd finally broken through the cloud cover — with a banger, not a whimper — though tentacles of the stuff still trailed from the wings like treacle.

And there I was, blinded by the light. Sightless, witless, breathless from it. And that was it. That's all she wrote. I could almost feel the ruby slippers (the bloody slippers!) sliding onto my feet, my heels clicking together. I leaned back, closed my eyes, and turned my face toward the sun.

Now I know where the phrase "rising above it" comes from. Forget the Bible. It's an ancient airline term.

* * *

My daughter is becoming increasingly independent. Last week she texted me from Omaha.

"What's my curfew?" she texted.

"What time zone are you in?" I texted back.

"American," she texted.

My daughter's sixteen. Where does a mother begin? With a beer and a shot, hopefully not to the head.

When I was sixteen I made the biggest decision of my life up until that point. And no, I'm not referring to the thumb-sucking thing, still working on it. I decided to put my Barbies in the neighborhood rummage sale.

It was an agonizing, soul-searching choice. Childhood's end and all that. Had I known that a half-century hence the blonde Barbie in the black-and-white-stripe swimsuit (whom I'd renamed Leslie) could send my daughter to two years of Community College — or pay her bail, whichever applied — I would've kept Ken, Leslie, and Midge living happily and alter-natively in the Dream House in my closet, listening to Vic Damone records on the cardboard hi-fi, watching Leslie on the cardboard Motorola, while their worth increased exponentially.

Not that my daughter is interested in college, community or otherwise. Her *apres*-high school plans involve one thing: travel. As in "out the front door."

I can relate. When my husband and I recently traveled to the UK, sandwiched between the Queen's Diamond Jubilee and the Olympics, in spite of record-rainfall and inappropriate footwear, we had a bloody great time. It wasn't so much the history, or the art, or the architecture, or even the pubs. It was the language. Everything sounds better in a British accent.

"Those dickwads at the next table?" I whispered to my husband over pints at the Pig and Fiddle. "A bunch of bloody wankers, but you'd never know it. It's the British accent! They sound smart! Even interesting! Even the bloody kids talk like this! Where do they get it from? It's like being in a bloody movie!"

Meanwhile, our daughter took advantage of our being on location across the pond to continue researching escape routes. She made it to Michigan, South Dakota, and the Canadian border before my parental radar kicked in. The only reason she didn't actually make it into Canadia, as she calls it, was lack of a passport.

"Hon," I whispered to my husband on the train to Scotland, "I forget, where's the Magnificent Mile?" I'd been searching for Free Cell on my husband's droid and managed to access my daughter's Facebook page.

"Chicago," said my husband, not in a British accent. "Hey, look! It's the Firth of Forth!"

Chicago?? This was my firth, er, first conscious awareness of the seriousness of our daughter's recon activities.

"What's the plan?" I always say, heading her off at the pass, whenever she books for the front door, iPod and bus card in hand.

"To not get kidnapped," she always says, oh-so-carefully inserting her earbuds.

That's another thing. While we were in England she pierced her left ear fourteen more times. At least now I know her eventual destination will be somewhere accessible only by bus or train. She'd never make it through airport security. I think her head is permanently tilted to the left, like her politics.

We're proud parents in that regard. Our daughter is a Yellow Dog Democrat down to her toenails. Make that Rainbow Dog Democrat. She's so open-minded you can practically hear the wind whistling through her ears. A sort of chiming sound, with all that hardware.

But that's what worries me. That wind. It brings out the meteorologist-in-a-helicopter mom in me.

"You need a plan after high school," I always say, whenever she breezes by the house to pick up clean underwear and forage for supplies.

I've been thinking about installing a time clock by the front door, having her punch in and out. I'll adjust her allowance according to how many actual man hours she spends on the premises.

"*Life Won't Give You An Allowance,*" I say, in upper-and-lower-case italics. "*You Have To Work. Go To College. Get A Job. Something.*"

"I choose Something," she says, flipping her hair like a cape and flying out the door. Again.

Next thing you know she's texting me from Altoona.

"What's for dinner?" she texts.

I have to google Altoona to find out where the bloody hell it is. There's at least two of them, one in Pennsylvania, one in Iowa. Where does a mother begin?

"I choose Iowa," I text back.

"???" she texts.

"For dinner," I text. "Let's meet halfway."

"Sounds like a plan," she texts back, not in a British accent.

UNNATURAL BASTERDS

My husband says you know you're getting older when you wake up in the morning and realize you've injured yourself sleeping. When he asked me what I wanted for Christmas, I told him a new vanity in the bathroom. The current one has four 500-watt lightbulbs lined up above the *top* of the mirror, and any serial killer knows you put vanity lights along the *side*, for crissakes. Things are bad enough without having to deal with the ghost of Jacob Marley first thing every day.

I knew I'd turned a corner when construction workers stopped whistling. It used to really piss me off when this happened, so I took to flipping them the bird. Which would really piss them off, making for some interesting exchanges.

Now it makes my entire month when some nearsighted asshole a half block away on a foggy day takes notice. Every once in a while a carload of hormone cases will discharge that distinct high-pitched jungle yelp in my direction, and I'll want *to* genuflect in gratitude. Usually this happens when the sun is going down and my back is turned (when glimpsed from behind from a moving vehicle, I can still pass) and my shades are on and my collar is up.

These days the only rise I seem to be able to get is from the garbage men, who wave gaily as they cruise the alley, probably because they're dumbfounded to find me standing upright given the number of beer and wine bottles they regularly find in our bins. The sound of our glass recycling hitting the inside of the truck resonates through the neighborhood like the Angelus. You can hear it a mile away.

I say, demon rum may not delay the aging process, but it delays having to think about it for the time being.

Still, taking my cue from the garbage men, and having nothing better to do, I decided to quit drinking. Stranger things have happened.

Actually I decided to quit drinking *for thirty days*. I'm "doing a thirty," as the saying goes.

This is day thirteen.

The first couple of days went relatively smoothly, and after a week of such madness, I felt so smug I wanted to celebrate with a case, er, glass of wine.

This seemed inappropriate somehow, so I decided to **Phone a Friend**. Except all my friends are soakers, I can't remember the last time I had a sober phone conversation, nix that idea.

So I decided to **Ask the Audience**.

"Hon ... " I purred to my husband in a voice I haven't used since the first Bush, " ... are you up for a little ... "

But I couldn't finish the sentence, I didn't want to raise his hopes. For me the word "celebration" is synonymous with "drunken orgy." Plus my husband's also doing a thirty — the family that detoxes together, etc. — what good is he.

All I had left was the *Fifty-Fifty* option. But deciding between a case of beer and a case of wine seemed, once again, inappropriate. I was at my wit's end. Literally. I had one wit left. And it was NA. What's a rummy to do?

So I took my remaining wit and my mineral water and located the nearest TV/Barcalounger combo, where I planted my dipsomaniacal ass and channeled Netflix. After seven hours of indecision, I Rokued "Two Weeks in Hell" and "Aryan Brotherhood Behind Bars" and settled in.

Sometime the following day I emerged, sober as the day I was born, which is pretty much the last time *that* happened. Between the Green Berets training program and a seemingly endless stream of humongous white tattooed shitbags, I'd had my fix. What this particular fix says about me, I don't want to know, but suffice to say I was loaded for beer, er, bear.

Which is a saying I utterly loathe. How about *loaded for Tea Partiers? loaded for teetotalers? loaded for tea drinkers?* Better yet, just make it *loaded* and let the party begin!

Believe me, "party" takes on a whole new meaning when you're doing a thirty (see above-mentioned Netflix selections). For decades I've been accustomed to raising a few whenever life presents one of those special occasions: birthdays, weddings, funerals, Thursdays. Raising a few juice boxes to toast the rising of the sun, or the arrival of the mail, just doesn't cut the mustard.

Speaking of which, I've had some interesting cravings these past two weeks, mustard being one. Also salt, oregano, tofu, PAM, Crest White Strips, and duct tape. Most unusual of all, I had an uncontrollable urge for an O'Doul's last Friday. Which, I'm happy to report, I was valiantly able to overcome, lest I actually be seen buying the stuff. My God, I still have my pride.

For an old boozer like myself, this is proving to be a cathartic experience. Not to mention lucrative. For the first time since becoming an adult, I suddenly have disposable income. Typically most of my income gets disposed down the nearest toilet — one doesn't *buy* beer, one *borrows* it — but now, here I am, swimming in cash! Frontcrawling, backstroking, deadmansfloating in it! What's a lush to do?

I opted for distraction. Is that one of the **Lifelines**? It should be.

I pocketed my booty and grabbed the car keys and headed out, not to my friendly neighborhood liquor store — my home away from home where everybody knows my name — but to my friendly neighborhood grocery store, where I planted myself in the produce section and harvested as many fresh citrus fruits (and a couple sticks of celery) as a shopping basket could hold.

Which I dutifully lugged through checkout while "My Name Is Wanda! How Can I Help You!" eyed the abundance of lemons and limes and peered at me as if to ask,

"Is that your final answer?"

No need to let Wanda in on my nasty little secret — *I utterly loathe fruit!* — so I gave her an acidic smile and loaded my purchases like wayward cue balls into my earth-friendly pockets.

Trust me on this, doing a thirty is *not* one of life's special occasions. When it comes to the excess citrus, I'm simply stockpiling for the next such special occasion: February! Because, as the saying goes, when life gives you lemons ... make margaritas!

Hola! Seventeen days to go.

* * *

Recently a good friend of ours was hospitalized with a stroke, and it gave those of us of a certain "era" pause. The good news is that our friend not only survived this frightening incident, but his prognosis is for a full recovery, in spite of his having spent an intense two weeks in surgical ICU with a hole in his head, from which a tube drained blood and spinal fluid away but, thankfully, not his excellent mind.

During those two weeks, his friends and family kept track of him on Caring Bridge, a website devoted to connecting people regarding health matters. There we could read daily journal entries, view photos, make tributes, or, if we chose, post to a guestbook.

By the time our friend was released from the hospital, his guestbook had risen to well over 200 posts, and given that he's a journalist, the posts from colleagues made for some great reading. These, alas, were scattered in amongst the usual plethora of God-centric outpourings, and after skimming a few dozen of the latter, I began to wonder if any of those people ever got up off their knees.

Still, I was reminded of W.C. Fields, a lifelong atheist, who, as the story goes, asked for a Bible on his deathbed. When questioned about this, he explained that he was just "looking for loopholes." Every man for himself when it comes to staring into the abyss, I say.

My husband, however, took great umbrage to the whole setup.

"When I keel over," he huffed, "don't you dare put me on fucking Caring Bridge."

"You won't have much say in the matter," I snorted, "you'll be fucking keeled over."

"You mean you won't honor my last wishes?" he demanded.

"Who says they're your last?" I retorted. "Miracles do happen."

"I don't believe in no miracles," he grumbled, "and neither do you."

"What does that have to do with letting your loved ones know the score?" I countered.

"I don't have any loved ones," he responded.

"You'd be surprised," I cautioned. "In a crisis, loved ones come out of the woodwork, there's a loved one under every rock."

"That's just what I mean," he complained. "I don't want some wayward loved one praying for me and 'sharing' it on some fucking website."

We paused momentarily in this grumbling / countering / complaining. Something had gotten my husband's goat, and now that the goat was out of the garage, it was too late to lower the door. Whatever.

After a while, my husband shrugged.

"Okay, have it your way," he acquiesced. "When I keel over, set up a Caring Bridge site, I don't give a fuck. But don't you dare allow a guestbook."

"I don't think you'll have a choice," I pointed out. "I think it's part of the package."

"*There will be no fucking guestbook!*" he inveighed. "It'll make me even sicker having to read all that drivel!"

"But think of our friend's guestbook," I mused, "there were so many great postings."

"That guy has talented, interesting, *intelligent* friends," he admonished, "their comments offset all that religious crap."

"Now you've gone and insulted our ... one friend," I warned. "I mean, you think after *your* brush with death, there'll be 237 posts on *your* guestbook? Think again, bubba."

"But I won't *have* a fucking guestbook!" he emphasized.

"We'll just see about that," I chided. "Come to think of it, maybe I'll open my *own* Caring Bridge site. Then well-wishers can sympathize with me for having to deal with a nudnik like you! Whatta ya think of them apples?"

"When I keel over," he muttered, "you'll be at my bedside 24-7, you won't have time to go around opening websites."

"Whatta ya mean, I'll be at your bedside?" I mimicked. "This is the ICU, don't forget. There's nothing I can do, my hands are tied, it's all up to the doctors now. I'll be down at the bar."

My husband stared at me.

"What?" I scoffed.

"Hospitals don't have bars," he sighed. "Cafeterias, coffee shops, gift shops ... no bars."

"Well what kind of fucked up deal is that?" I bellyached. "Who needs coffee at a time like this? A couple stiff bumps is more like it."

"I'd say you got a couple stiff bumps," he observed, "on your head."

Which brought us back around to the recent matter involving our *friend's* head, which gave us pause, which made us feel like a couple of muttering / mimicking / bellyaching assholes for carrying on while our friend was recovering from having just spent two weeks in ICU with a hole in his head, not to be confused with the holes in *our* heads which, I might add, have been there considerably longer and show no signs of closing up any time soon.

I stood up. Did I mention we'd been sitting around the Christmas tree?

"Truce?" I asked.

"For instance?" he wondered.

"How's about a little Christmas cheer?" I offered.

"How's about, *Two-Four-Six-Eight! Meetcha at the Pearly Gate!*" he suggested.

"That's not what I meant," I replied. "Besides, you don't believe in no pearly gate."

"I'm talking about a drink," he corrected. "There's gotta be a drink by that name."

"I'll google it," I promised. "In the meantime, how's about a couple stiff bumps?"

"Just what the doctor ordered," he agreed, and resumed Christmas-tree-gazing.

Meanwhile, out in the starless night, the snow careened mercilessly around a nearby streetlight.

Pearly Gate

2 oz single malt scotch (Lagavulin if you have the dinero)

1 oz Amontillado (approx. 1/2000 of a cask)

1 tbs chocolate syrup

1 tsp coffee

dash sea salt

ice

Stir. Sip. Pray. Repeat.

* * *

The neighbors are getting a divorce.

"Lucky bastards," says my husband.

I don't think luck has anything to do with it. I think it's the househusband.

Call me Old School, there's something unnatural about a househusband. It goes against the laws of physics. I grew up with a house*wife*. Who wore house*dresses*, who did house*work*, who ran a house*hold*. Here's the physics part: an apron (not to mention a babushka) just doesn't look the same on a guy.

Of course aprons and babushkas are Old School, right up there alongside ringer washers and party lines and 35-cents-a-gallon gasoline. Just the same, the househusband next door circumvented the babushka issue by going bald. I don't mean he *went* bald, I mean he *shaved* himself bald. This happened just after the divorce notice appeared in the newspaper, another iconic item on its way to that Old School in the Sky.

One day I'm on my way out to the garage when I glance toward our twenty-foot privacy fence and a sudden beam of light singes my retina. I peer through the periscope and determine the source: it's the sun reflecting off the next-door househusband's newly shaved head.

I call my husband. He doesn't answer, he's at *work*. I lower the drawbridge, cross the moat, throw some raw meat to the guard dogs, and drive away in a cloud of dust, ignoring the friendly wave of the househusband across the alley hanging out the wash. I think he had a couple of clothespins in his mouth.

We moved into this fortress fifteen years ago, and since then, househusbands have cropped up around the neighborhood like creeping charlie. There's the bald one next door, the one across the street, the one down the block, and the one across the alley with the clothespins, who replaced the one who moved away and was the forerunner of the whole infestation.

Meanwhile, back in the Jeep, I careen to a stop in front of the liquor store, run inside, and call my husband. This time he answers.

"I'm fucking freezing!" I say.

"It's over 70," he says, "I walked to work."

"That's what I *mean!*" I say. "You walked to *work*! You're at *work*!"

"Where are *you?*" he says.

"In the Beer Cave!" say I.

"That's why you're fucking freezing," says he. Then he says, "You caved."

My husband and I have been on this low-alcohol diet for a few months: we only drink when absolutely necessary. For him that means holidays and special occasions. For me that means when I'm not sleeping.

"It's the neighbors!" I say. "The ones getting the divorce!"

"Lucky bastards," says my husband.

"Never mind that!" I say. "It's the househusband! He's fucking bald!"

That stops my husband in his tracks. Nothing gets a guy's attention like another guy's hair loss.

"Whatta ya mean, 'bald?'" says my husband.

"As in 'no hair!'" I say. "As in Lightbulb City!"

"But ... " says my husband.

You have to realize the guy we're talking about is in his thirties. He's a Cub Scout. A Little Leaguer. A small fry. A fetus. A week ago he had a full head of hair.

"It's obvious!" I say. "He shaved his head!"

"But why?" says my husband. "What for?"

"In fucking protest!" I say. "His heart's broken! His life's over! He's staring into the abyss!"

"I highly doubt it," says my husband.

A week ago, when the fetus had hair, I was repositioning the telescope one evening and accidentally discovered him and a blonde drinking wine and eating takeout at his kitchen table. Lo mein. With chopsticks. His wife's a brunette.

His wife's also a doctor. As in MD, as in always working, as in took time off for a couple of kids and got right back in the saddle, as in *in need of a wife*.

Enter, your friendly neighborhood househusband.

These househusbands must have some online community somewhere, some chatroom in the cloud, where they gather regularly and swap gossip and life stories and microwave recipes, and share information re up-and-coming neighborhoods targeted for infiltration. "Househusband's List," "Househusbands Anonymous," something like that.

Except there's nothing anonymous about these guys. They're fucking proud of their stay-at-home status. They wear it like a badge of honor. Make that jockstrap of honor.

"You're a real asshole," said my husband.

This was later that same day, following the Beer Caving incident. The temperature had also caved, never mind this was mid-May and earlier it had warmed up enough to thaw out the birdbath. By now the local robins are hip to the scene. As soon as they feel the plunge coming on, they immediately take wing, lest they be frozen to the concrete mid-bath.

My husband and I were sitting in our parkas in the living room, feeding the fire, drinking our respective drinks, eating Progresso Minestrone Soup and Old Dutch Fat Free Pretzel Twists. It'd been my turn to cook dinner. I'd already checked in with the telescope, but Telly Savalas had taken to drawing his drapes.

"I am not an asshole," I said. "I am a natural woman."

"Natural disaster maybe," said my husband, slurping soup and Amanda Marie's Just Peachy Detox Tea.

"Just think about it," I said. "Could you see *yourself* hanging out in the house all day? Watering plants? Watching *Dr. Phil*? Not answering the phone for fear of robo calls?"

"Sounds good to me," said my husband. "But who'd pay for all this? Who'd foot the bill? Who'd bring home the bacon?"

"First of all," I said, "we're vegetarians. And B, I have a job."

"Yeah, right," said my husband. "You make the same as you did in 1977 when you were just another lounge act trying to break into waitressing."

"I've adjusted for inflation," I said.

"The only thing inflated around here is our waistlines," said my husband.

"Speak for yourself," I said, popping another Fat Free Twist and washing it down with Corona.

"Besides," I said, "if you had all that free time, you might end up like Mr. Househusband next door, clattering around your empty house, shaving your empty head, eating cheap Chinese with some empty blonde."

"Lucky bastard," said my husband, and stared into the fire.

Just then, a log fell.

I'm trying not to think of The Fire. Last week people down in The City could smell the smoke I'm trying to think of something other than all those animals and birds, all that old-growth pine, all that sacred wilderness.

I wonder what's going through the mind of the dickwad whose campfire started this disaster. Was he drunk? on his cell phone? spanking the monkey?

A fire of this magnitude hasn't occurred in the border country for nearly a hundred years. They say we were due, it would've happened sooner or later, it was inevitable, especially after the blowdown of '99. A powder keg, they called it. Explosive. This is Mother Nature, after all, just doing her thing.

Well, hey. I'm as capable as the next guy of comprehending the process by which the boreal forest rejuvenates itself. Up at the cabin we're surrounded by jack pine and black spruce, both fire-dependent species. We collect jack pine cones, they're tucked everywhere into the cabin's nooks and crannies, tight little fists holding a secret.

But none of that helps. I'm overwhelmed. I can't get beyond the catastrophic violence and devastation and death.

When my family asks what I want for Mother's Day, I say, I want to go to the cabin. And so I do, just me and the husky. I can see the smoke as I drive up the shore, I can smell it. When I finally turn off the car and step into the yard, I'm acutely aware that it's out there, some forty or fifty miles northwest of where I stand: The Fire.

This awareness is behind everything I do, everywhere I go, all the familiar rituals and activities, all the long weekend. I'm not worried about our dream going up in smoke, but I can't stop thinking of all those others who weren't so lucky. Somehow it comforts me to be there, in the same neck of the woods, however distant, however safe.

Then, late Sunday night: The Storm. The husky slinks up beside me in the dark, quivering with terror, and my cocoon of woodsmoke-scented quilts morphs into a Vibra Bed. We huddle together under the too-low ceiling while the thunder crashes and the windows tremble in their frames and the Canadian Shield reverberates beneath us and lightning transforms midnight into noon.

It comes in waves and lasts for hours. I try to tell the husky this is a good thing. I tell her about the birds and the bears and the deer, about the flames like dragonfire, the trees like matchsticks burning. I try to tell her about the rain the rain the rain. I whisper into her ear, fur tickling my lips. Only she's not buying. Won't be lulled. Her fear of storms is deep and visceral and ancient.

But I can do something she can't. I have a secret. I can envision the next moment, the next hour, the next morning. This too shall pass. The storm, the fire. I can envision a future. Which I try, keep trying, to do. While the bed shimmies and the windows shake and the storm rampages on. Until, good little zen dog that she is, the husky pulls me back, into the only moment she knows. Into the now, into the present. Where we remain for the duration, huddled together, while all around us the woods fills up with ghosts.

ACTS OF GOD

The Boundary Waters are on fire again. An act of God this time. In the form of a lightning bolt, what else. You'd think by now God would've gotten a little more creative.

It started with a high pressure area over the Lake, which lasted for a week, another miracle of the first magnitude, this being September. But miracles in these parts are few and far, the pressure was on, something had to give.

"No more Mr. Nice Guy!" booms God, and throws down the above-mentioned lightning bolt and hauls out the marshmallows.

The fire is the biggest in state history, bigger even than the last record-breaking BWCA fire, the one caused by an act of man. The man in question was eventually outed, and the story ended when he offed himself, apparently out of despair over the devastation he'd brought about. That and the felony lawsuit the feds slapped on his sad ass.

You can run, but you can't hide.

The smoke from the Pagami Creek Fire can be seen from space. It looks like some humongous supersizer is sitting just below the North Pole blowing a humongous blunt toward Chicago. It might be Santa, but more than likely it's that wily ol' God.

"Yeah, but I didn't inhale!" booms God, deftly covering his humongous ass once again.

People in Chicago are pissed. I mean, more so than usual.

Much like New Yorkers, Chicagoans tend to forget there's another reality beyond the Windy City's limits. As opposed to Angelinos, whose sense of reality bends the boundaries of the time/space continuum and astral projects them into alternate universes on a regular weekly basis, beginning September 26th at 8 p.m. Eastern / 7 Central.

Angelinos ... ya gotta love 'em. But God doesn't. Does the word "earthquake" mean anything to you? How about Santa Ana winds? wildfires? mudslides? *Arnold Schwarzenegger?*

You can run, but you can't hide. I'm telling you, there's nowhere left to go.

Used to be Up North was a relative safe zone, unless you happen to be classified as a game animal, but don't get me started. Suffice to say that for the human species, at least, Up North has traditionally been a sort of Switzerland of the midsection, the remoteness and the weather keeping the riffraff out and the IQs down.

But then God moves in, there goes the neighborhood.

By the time God finally dragged his humongous ass Up North, he'd apparently run out of cutting edge ideas and was forced to resort to the old tried and true biblical ravages of pestilence, locusts, and lightning bolts. *Oh my!* Translation: lyme disease, mosquitoes, and supersized forest fires.

Apparently God hates pretty much everyone.

I just checked, and as of this morning, the winds have shifted and the fire is headed for Canada. I trust the Border Patrol is on top of things.

After 9/11, the gub'ment suddenly discovered our remote little corner of the world, and the Border Patrol have been zipping around these backwoods in their little Shriner cars for the past ten years or so, dodging moose and bear and jackpine savages, and diligently adding to the tax base, the roadkill count, and the bar bill over at My Sister's Place, one of the local watering holes.

Rumor has it that a few years back a pair of BPs donned Sherlock Holmes hats and managed to track a couple of suspicious characters carrying suspicious packages, who'd somehow managed to make it across the Pigeon River and enter the good ol' U.S. of A. illegally, before spending a fortnight wandering in the wilderness, *a.k.a.* the Boundary Waters, like Moses looking for a way out.

The way out being Highway 61, our local backstreet, where a passing motorist discovered said suspicious characters prostrate on the shoulder, thumbs extended, heads resting on the suspicious packages, which turned out to be backpacks stuffed with the latest REI camping gear the hapless Canucks had recently purchased up in Thunder Bay. Maybe next time they'll throw in a couple of GPS units.

The "suspects" were apprehended and questioned by the BPs, then promptly dispatched to the border crossing, where they were last seen hiking along Highway 61 back into Canada, thumbs extended, shouting every last verse of "Positively 4th Street" back at the good ol' U.S. of A. at the top of their lungs, with feeling.

I'd like to shout every last verse of "Positively 4th Street" back at God at the top of my lungs with feeling. I'd just like to come out once and scream it. I mean, he's got a lot of nerve. All around him 100,000 acres of wilderness and all its inhabitants are going up in smoke, and he just stands there, humongous hands on humongous hips, grinning. I wish that for just one time he could stand inside my shoes. He'd know what a drag it is to see him.

* * *

I was finishing up a run the other morning — it's true, occasionally I'm up before noon — when a red fox trotted across the road in front of me. He was sleek and magnificent in the April sun, his red bush of a tail following like a flag, and suddenly I felt the universe *click!* into benevolent compliance all around me.

I continued my run, and the feeling of goodwill was so strong that I did something completely out of character. Swallowing my habitual cud of misanthropy, I opened up to a fellow human being: I shared my experience with a nearby cemetery worker.

Did I mention I was running in the cemetery?

"Ya, vell, ve no like da fockses," she shared back in heavily-accented English, shaking her gray head ruefully. "Day keel da baybays of da geeses, not so many baybays for two, tree years now."

I stared at her, mouth agape — I'd been running, after all — as the bubble of cosmic altruism enveloping me imploded with an audible *pwoof!* So much for the universe clicking into compliance.

Speaking of which.

After being one of the last holdouts on the planet, and in an effort to step back from the abyss over which I've been teetering for two, tree decades now, I finally joined Facebook. Hold the applause. I can't say exactly why I caved, except I glanced at my Free Cell stats and realized my total number of games played was nearing six figures. And that's just the last six months. Clearly I needed an intervention.

So I laid in a supply of whiskey, bolted the door of my study, sat down at my computer, and googled Facebook. Nine hours later the whiskey was gone, and I'd gotten as far as my name. So I summoned my daughter. Let it be known that I went to my daughter as a last resort, I still have my motherly pride. Which is pretty much all I have left in the motherly department.

It took my daughter four-and-a-half minutes to sign me up, another four-and-a-half to cancel her own account and open a new one under a pseudonym. Heaven forbid I should stalk, er, run into her on Facebook and request that she be my friend.

An oxymoron if ever there was.

So I've been on Facebook for a little over a week now, and I'm proud to say I have eight friends. Applause! Which is more than I have in real life, go figure. My daughter has 794. On her *new* account. She's also been after me to "like" something, to which I say, you can lead a horse to water, but you can't make her like it.

"You know me," I neighed to her in a friendly manner, "I don't like anything. Last time I liked something was 1967."

"I like over 3,000 things," she said, adjusting an earbud and texting her boyfriend on her smartphone.

I stared at her, mouth agape — I'd been surfing Facebook, after all — as another ad for AARP popped into view on the right-hand side of my screen.

Here's how it works: the middle-schoolers who run Face-book insist on a legitimate birthdate before granting you an account, thereby enabling some algorithm in the sky, er, cloud to bombard you with age-appropriate advertisements in the hopes that you might "like" something. Ever since joining this cult, I've been plagued with ads for false teeth, hair loss remedies, and AARP paraphernalia, not to mention long-term care insurance and Living Wills. I expect an ad for cemetery plots to pop up at any second.

That's another thing: once you're on Facebook, you've entered the Land of the Present Tense. You're expected to give a minute-by-minute play-by-play of your oh-so-interesting never-a-dull-moment life. It's called "What's on your mind?" For example, you might post:

"This morning I took an awesome dump!"

Seven seconds later, you find out five people "liked" this. One even commented:

"Way to 'go!' LOL!"

Next thing you know, an ad for Kaopectate pops up on your screen at the top of the list, cutting in front of the 173 "mutual friends of friends" who've been clamoring to be *your* friend, or else. God forbid you should "Not Now" one of these mutuals and have your refusal come back to bite you in the virtual ass when you least expect it:

"So *now* you're requesting to be *my* friend?!? What's up with *that?!?* You *'Not Nowed'* me three months ago, dickhead!! Eat shit!!"

Your social network can start to look like a Silly String incident.

So last night I was on Facebook stalking, er, looking up old boyfriends so I could check out what shape their wives were in, when I noticed my daughter's name in the chat column with a green dot. Which means she was surfing. Chat column ... green dots ... surfing ... isn't it just too cool how hip I'm becoming? After only one week?!? Two seconds later a little message box popped up:

"mom when r u going 2 take me prom shopping"

My scalp tingled with anticipation. My daughter's going to the prom, she needs me! Mostly to drive her to the mall and pay for everything, but still. I cracked my knuckles and started typing:

"Well imagine this! Here we are engaged in conversation on Facebook! Did you ever think you'd see the day? BTW, have you seen the TV remote? Never mind, let's not waste valuable space in this precious little box on such minutiae! Anyhoo ... I was just counting my friends to see if anyone had unfriended me yet, when I noticed your green dot, and next thing you know, here you are! You messaged me! I'm so honored I could..."

At this point I'd overflowed the message box and had to scroll back to the top to reacquaint myself with the question.

" ... get carried away! That IS my name after all! Ha ha! Anyhoo ... how's about I swing by and pick you up after school on Tuesday, and we head on over to Dave's Bridal Barne? Does that work for you, sweetiepie?"

I sent the message and poured another four fingers of whiskey. Thirty seconds later my daughter's reply appeared:

"its dawns bridal shoppe. tuesday ok. DONT COME 2 SCHOOL!! ill meet u there"

I made a mental note to start using textspeak whenever I'm in the message box, then checked out another wife. Whoo-ee, I'll bet Bosco (not his real name) is kicking himself in the nuts right about now for letting a hip focks like me get away!

I shot the last finger of whiskey and made another mental note to go twice around the cemetery next time. As they say, use it or lose it. Which is pretty much how I feel about joining Facebook. The experience has been only slightly less traumatic than a root canal, and I got mine back in the days when whiskey was still an anesthetic option.

* * *

Back in my late twenties, when my main interests in life were getting stoned and playing guitar, I woke up one morning with a life-altering toothache — you know what I'm talking about — and a friend of mine referred me to a friend of hers whom she referred to as the Hippie Dippie Dentist. I showed up in his chair one morning, he turned on the gas and KQ, I left a month later with a refurbished mouth and an open-ended prescription for Tylenol Three. He wasn't called the Hippie Dippie Dentist for nothing.

Fast forward a few more months. Make that a year. First, a confession.

In those bright shining days of my youth, before presbyopia and hot flashes and the ongoing root canal of parenthood, when I could still transport all my worldly possessions to a new apartment in two, tree carloads, I went through a period of irresponsibility. Okay, major irresponsibility. I existed outside the box. I didn't believe certain aspects of society applied to me.

For example: I had the habit of ignoring parking tickets. I mean, they just didn't figure into my overall worldview. I figured the cops had better things to do than worry about an arch criminal such as myself, so I'd peel the tickets off the windshield and file them away into the far recesses of the back seat. It all seemed harmless enough and went on for some time, until … but that's a whole other story in which a horse figures prominently.

I also had the habit of filing away into the far recesses of my desk drawer certain questionable pieces of mail that interfered with the well-being of my psyche. My dental bill was one of them. No excuses, I was an asshole. Okay, major asshole. But at the time, I saw myself as a quasi-dropout, one of the disenfranchised, basically invisible. I shopped at Rag Stock, let my body hair grow, got stoned on an as-needed basis (read: daily), didn't own a phone or a television or a credit card or eat meat. I rarely drank alcohol because I was a pot-snob.

What happened was this: the Hippie Dippie Dentist began showing up at my gigs.

Did I mention I was a local counter-culture guitar hero?

I'd be at a gig, tuning my E-string, adjusting the mic, and I'd look up through a haze of smoke and there he'd be, front and center at one of those frisbee-sized tables, sucking down Black Russians and glaring daggers at me. Make that drill bits. He never said anything, just glared and sucked. He might've been stoned, maybe he carried a portable nitrous oxide pump in his pants. Feeling guilty, I never spoke to him, either, and we went on for some time like this, two silent figments of our respective imaginations circling one another through a tangle of smoky nightspots around town.

And then, one night, he disappeared. Just like that. I never saw him again, never got another dental bill.

What I got was a summons, to appear in small claims court.

This should've rattled a normal person. But I was cool. Disenfranchised. Invisible. I set my alarm clock to within an inch of its life, caught a bus downtown to the courthouse, found courtroom number four, settled back and waited for my number to be up.

When the judge told me to approach, I approached. When he asked me to verify the details of the charge, I verified. When he asked me how I pleaded, I said *Guilty*, then I added *I guess*. When he asked me what I was going to do to rectify the situation, I paused, then shrugged. He looked down at me over the top of his glasses and asked me to explain. I shrugged again. He paused, then asked me if I intended to pay off this debt. I said *Probably not*. He said *You're not going to make good on this?* I said *No*, then I added *Sir*. I wanted to make that *Your Holiness*, but wisely reconsidered. Then the judge said, *I have no choice but to render judgment against you in this matter, please see the bailiff,* and he shook his head. I'd like to believe the corners of his mouth turned up just a wee bit, but more likely it was acid reflux.

What I do know is that in spite of the patina of former dirtball that muddied my aura, my husband hooked up with me anyway. Solid citizen that he is, he must've been feverish at the time. Temporarily insane. Horny.

Of course this didn't happen until much later, and by then my life had changed yet again. But the statute of limitations must have run out or something — who am I kidding, it was a fucking miracle — because I emerged from the fog of my brilliant youth with a better-than-average credit rating. And a goldcapped root canal that's still in my head, last time I checked.

SMOKE

What do you do when your kid runs away? I mean, before the champagne?

First, you get down on your knees. And clean. When the kid Zambonied through the house stuffing as much shit as she could fit into a dozen paper bags, she left a bit of a mess in her wake.

Which is the second thing you do. You hold a wake. That's where the champagne comes in.

Third thing, you put out a contract. On God. Not that you believe all that bullshit. It's just you have to cover all the bases, you have to do something.

What you did was, thirteen years ago — a lifetime ago — you opened your door. I mean, there was a baby on your doorstep, what's a mensch to do? At the time you didn't know you were a mensch. You just thought you were a putz. This was before you became a schmuck.

It wasn't the baby's fault, it wasn't your fault, but none of that mattered in the end. It all imploded, and the baby blamed you. She had to blame someone, you were all she had.

Actually, it wasn't a baby on your doorstep, it was a little kid. Who didn't stay little for long. Meanwhile, you became littler and littler until you disappeared altogether.

When you finally reappeared, you found yourself down on your knees, cleaning. With no memory of how you got there and nothing to show for it. Except in the mirror. Where thirteen years had somehow turned into thirty.

What do you do when the house is cleaned and the hangover tamed and the contract notarized? You go to a meeting. With your husband. Did I mention there's another schmuck in this story?

So anyways, youse two schmucks kiss the dog and lock the door and drive through a blizzard in below-zero dark and almost get sideswiped by a Bud truck and eventually find yourselves out on Highway 53, sitting around a table under fluorescent lights, with eighteen other people in parkas drinking Pepsi and eating pizza that may or may not be real. The table is huge. So are most of the people.

Turns out these people regularly open their doors to babies of all sizes and ages, they do it for a living. One couple has eight kids, another ten, the rest have at least four or five apiece. Which is how many bottles of Bud you wish you had.

So they drink their Pepsi and wipe their foreheads and swap their stories — *kids playing with scissors with axes with fires with knives* — and shake their heads as if to say *"Whatchagonnado?"* and stuff in more pizza, and it begins to dawn on youse two schmucks dat you're in da wrong meetin', dat dere *ain't* no meetin', dere *ain't* no club for da likes a youse two.

So youse make your move, youse make your getaway, only youse have to climb over four or five people to do so, but eventually youse get to the door and youse make your exit, mouths full of parka fur dat may or may not be real.

What do you do when you come to a fork in the road?

Actually you keep finding forks — and spoons and knives and mummified sandwiches — under the couch in the spare room where the kid's been squatting for the past few years.

It occurs to you you should've kept up with the cleaning and vacuuming, but you thought that was the housekeeper's bailiwick. You forgot about the clause in the housekeeper's contract that excluded skeletons in closets. Or under furniture, apparently.

Long before making her getaway, the kid moved out of her bedroom into the spare room because, she said, there were too many goblins under her bed.

Spare room. Spare kid. It was a metaphorical move.

You don't know from goblins. But there are so many skeletons around you could open an osteological museum. You think about this as you watch the new moon sidle up from the treeline. It's a comma. An apostrophe. A parenthesis. A single quote. Like the one about the fork.

How does it go again? What do you do when you come to a fork in the road? You take it. I mean, you know a fork when you see one.

* * *

The other day I got carded. At Target. For trying to buy a package of lighters. I stared aghast at the twelve-year-old cashier, who clicked her tongue ring and enlightened me:

"Becaushe of underage schmoking."

I stared, not only aghast, but agape. Her name badge said "Natalee."

"Open your eyes, Natalee," I instructed. "The last time I got carded was during the Nixon administration!"

"Who?" Natalee clicked, and swiped my driver's license.

I added agog to the list.

"The Shtate wansh a record of who buysh lightersh," Natalee clicked further, rolling her eyes.

I waited patiently while she freed some of her lashes from an eyebrow ring, and fought a sudden overpowering urge to share:

"I'm buying these lighters, Natalee, because I'm really into candles and fires, and everybody knows you can't be too thin or too rich or have too many candles or fires, and there's this seventeen-year-old who stops by my house every few days when I'm not there to shower and eat and change clothes and case the joint for any cash or credit cards or car keys or jewelry that might be lying around, and also any lighters, because the State wants to keep lighters out of the hands of underage kids because everybody knows there's a problem with underage schmoking, er, smoking, and this seventeen-year-old smokes anything that can be lit, Natalee, which pretty much describes the state she's been in for the past twelve to eighteen months, not to be confused with the state where we live, which state, as stated, wants to keep lighters out of the hands of seventeen-year-olds, so every fucking lighter in my house is gone, Natalee, fucking gone, so I started hiding matches from my matchbook collection from back in the seventies when I was a local culture hero down in The City, but lately my senior moments are morphing into senior months and I can't remember where the fuck I hid the fucking matches from my matchbook collection, and did I mention the seventeen-year-old got bored with cutting and piercing and tattooing herself, so she dropped out of high school and took up couch-surfing and skyway-walking and coffee-shopping with some dirtbag named Molly?, and who the fuck is this Molly anyway?, but never mind, this seventeen-year-old also took up pawnshopping, with a little help from the jewelry she palmed from my jewelry box a few weeks back when I had H1N1 and lay half dead in a nearby bed hallucinating with fever, thus this particular purchash, er, purchase, Natalee, for which you have duly carded me, although I may be back because, as also stated, there's a good chance I won't remember where the fuck I hid any of them, the matches, that is, and it's a brave new world, Natalee, a brave new fucking world, not that I'd expect you to grasp any literary reference I might throw your way."

But I didn't. Share.

Instead I paid for the lighters and thanked Natalee and drove home and hid them all carefully and then changed the locks on all my doors.

Which is why I've spent the last day-and-a-half searching the joint for my new house keys, and also something to light my fire, or my candles, whichever proves more appropriate depending on the weather, because even though it's shpring, er, spring, given the state I'm in, I'm waiting for god-knows-what to monsoon through at any moment.

It's never Wisconsin. Or Utah. Or Texas. It's never Iowa or Connecticut. It's always only one state, which isn't even a state any more, it's a concept.

I picture a fortune-teller in a fortune-telling booth gazing into a crystal ball behind a curtain.

"You're going on a long journey," says the fortune-teller. "It's your destiny, your karma, your vision quest, whatever. It's no mystery, baby, you're going to California. Four days by land, three hours by air, no sea option. I take Visa."

Back in the day, a friend of mine used to paraphrase Steinbeck: if you picked up the country like a pizza pan and tipped it, all the loose olives would end up in California.

Pizza pan, album cover, Ouija Board, whatever. These days you could pick up the entire fucking planet, the same thing would happen.

So there I am, just hanging out, minding my own business, relaxing into my new pointless purposeless lifestyle (translation: I'm prostrate in the Barcalounger torpedoing through a *Breaking Bad* marathon on Netflix), when I get a text. I leave Walter White staring indefinitely at an eyeball in his suitcase, and pick up my phone.

It's a photo. Of a damselfly. In the sun. On the sand.

I live in a place where, if you picked it up and tipped it slightly, nothing would happen. *Nada.* Everyone and everything is mired in twelve feet of snow, baby, nobody's goin' nowhere, April notwithstanding.

Like the other day, I'd just strapped myself into the cockpit of the Barcalounger to rejoin Walter, when an enormous *KA-BAM!!* shook the house to its foundation. And no, it wasn't a couple of planes colliding head-on over the neighborhood (Season 2, Episode 13). It was a glacial ice plate plummeting from our three-story roof onto the front patio. Make that *former* front patio.

So the damselfly in the sun on the sand was my first clue.

The second was the phone it was sent from.

. . .

There's a massive antique heating oil tank sitting in a far corner of our basement, somewhere along the line someone painted it silver. It's empty, hasn't been in use for decades, and reverberates resoundingly if you knock on it. I like to picture it up at the cabin, back in the woods somewhere, like some late model dinosaur keeping watch. But it's lived in the basement of our century-old house since the Great Depression, it ain't goin' nowhere.

A small mountain range of boxes sits beside the tank. My husband moved them there on the downlow one night last week, from the last place our daughter had been staying. Despite her couch-surfer-girl MO, our daughter has managed to accrue some baggage, so when circumstances necessitated that she once again find a new living situation, she called for backup from the family moving and storage company. I mean, what's a father for?

Meanwhile, having lightened her load considerably, our daughter stuffed as much as she could into an oversized purse and a backpack, said she'd be by to reclaim the rest of it soon, and headed for another couch. A friend of a friend's, she said. Although she neglected to mention one minor detail: the precise GPS location of this couch.

Incense and cigarettes and weed ... wasn't that some old sixties song? Whatever, that's what our basement smells like now. I should roll up my sleeves and go through that pile of boxes and dig out all the washable stuff and have at it. Like that might help, like that might change anything. I mean, what's a mother for?

Except I keep putting it off. I know a Pandora when I smell one.

Our daughter has been couch-surfing for a couple of years.

It started at home, when she vacated her blue-and-yellow bedroom during sophomore year to set up camp in the TV room. She grooved on that, so halfway through junior year, she packed up a few essentials, gave the finger to everything else, and headed out the front door to surf the larger world.

So much for high school. Home. Apple pie. Roku-on-demand. She'd had enough. Enough of one thing, anyway. But nowhere near enough of something else.

That's all she wrote. Unless she needed money.

It was the beginning of a beautiful downfall.

So I stared at the damselfly on my phone, and didn't understand.

Then a few hours later, I got another text, a photo of Mount Rushmore. Then another, a herd of curly sheep. Then yesterday, it was the Rockies. With an unfamiliar car in the foreground, a familiar purse lying on its hood.

Now I understand. Now I know. But I already know too much. Now I just want to be dumb — as a stone, a stoner, a couch, a dinosaur.

So I picture something else. I picture a journey, a destiny, a karma, a vision quest. After the snow recedes, after the *Aha!* realization that snow does not cover the entire fucking planet, after the Badlands and the Canyon and the mountains and the desert, I picture this:

Late afternoon, condor drifting overhead, wildflowers waving from the roadside, and a white late model Mustang convertible crests a hill in the yellow sun toward the blue horizon of ocean, trailing its shadow like an ellipsis.

You know that ubiquitous smoky atmosphere that periodically envelops Southern Cali? That's not wildfires, baby. It's the smell of bridges burning.

BACK TO THE GARDEN

(No fish in the house now. No birds. No reptiles, no fur-bearers, no pre-adult humanoids. The food chain has been disrupted. I'm talking to the plants.)

A ctually I've been talking to plants since the Nixon administration, since my first significant botanical relationship. You know the one, all you botanists of a certain era.

There I am at the U, institution of higher learning, just some smalltown Iron Range escapee with a new set of matching Samsonite, all set to get me some of that learning. Meanwhile, all hell is breaking loose outside my dorm room window — sit-ins, protests, take-overs, strikes — believe me, Mother never said there would be days like *this*.

What Mother *said* was,

"A girl can always use a good wig."

She was preparing me for my Big College Adventure, helping me fill those three pieces of matching Samsonite, secretly congratulating herself on her two-down-one-to-go success ratio in drop-kicking the fledglings out of the nest.

Never mind Mother never went to college herself. She was a member of the League of Women Voters, owned a set of Patty Berg golf clubs, made groovy personalized place cards when it was her turn for Bridge Club, and sold Beauty Counselor to the local miners' wives when she wasn't cooking, cleaning, drawing on lips and eyebrows, or drop-kicking fledglings out of nests.

It was 1969. Mother was a Modern Woman. Jackie Onassis would be proud.

So there I am, fresh out of some open pit mine, shitting bricks and trailing ore dust, hauling a three-piece matched set of psychedelic blue-flowered luggage stuffed with mix-and-match Bobbie Brooks skirt sets and a blonde pixie wig across a campus of 50,000 students, half of them stoned.

As quick as you can say LSMFT, I figured out three things: nobody had matching luggage; nobody had matching clothes; nobody had a matching wig. I had all three. I was nobody.

What's a girl to do? I stuffed the luggage under my dorm room bed and started eating.

By the end of my first week I'd gained twenty pounds, discovered Camel straights, opened up an account at the Harvard Market on Washington Avenue so I'd never run out of Screaming Yellow Zonkers, and hitchhiked downtown to a new store, Ragstock, where I traded the Bobbie Brooks for a handful of oversized gabardine women's suit jackets from the forties and an Army surplus backpack.

I saved the wig for emergencies.

Little did I know that Life from then on would be nothing but a continuing series of emergencies of varying degrees of magnitude, one after another after another, punctuated by sporadic interludes of unspeakable bliss, till death do us part.

As for higher learning, I graduated *magna cum laude* in

"higher." But the "learning" took a nosedive the moment I showed up for Psychology 101 and took a look around the auditorium at my 5,000 fellow classmates.

When I wasn't protesting or striking or sitting-in or taking-over, I was lounging around somebody's dorm room in the honeymoon throes of that first botanical relationship, playing *Abbey Road* backwards in the company of other young botanists, searching for answers to that ultimate existential question: *is Paul dead?*

After a few hours of this, and having reached no definitive conclusion, we'd give in to that universal urge rampant in all young girls away from home for the first time: *LET'S EAT SOMETHING!! LET'S EAT IT NOW!! LET'S EAT A LOT OF IT!!*

We'd hitch up our bell bottoms, throw on our ponchos, and head on over to the nearest Bridgeman's, where we'd park ourselves in a corner booth and order Bridgeman Barges all around. Our table looked like a jam-up at the Upper St. Anthony Falls Lock and Dam a few miles upriver.

But as difficult as it was to maneuver oneself around a 500-acre campus after consuming a riverboat of ice cream and toppings the memory of which turns me pea green with nausea to this day, it was even more difficult to make one's way unaffected through the growing maelstrom of anger and unrest that was College 1969.

Even for a displaced nobody from the Iron Range.

The blinders were off. If not the wig. I had arrived in my *Life*.

* * *

In those days we all smoked. It was a prerequisite.

I'd be sitting in class taking notes on *Moby Dick*, Prufrock, the moon illusion, and everyone would be smoking, including the prof. Some limpdicks would ash into their cigarette packs, but most of us just ashed off the side of our desks and ground the butt into the floor. College 1969 was basically an enormous ashtray.

You felt like you were crawling through your life in some kind of fog anyway, the smoke haze was fitting, poetic even. Half the guys you grew up with were crawling through some jungle haze on the other side of the planet, or trying to figure out how to get the hell out of it, everything seemed connected.

Only it wasn't.

With my blue suede clogs and six-inch hoops and Mexican shoulder bag crammed with Shakespeare and Yardley of London, I was about as connected to a jungle in Southeast Asia as I was to Piccadilly Circus, or George Harrison, my favorite Beatle.

Which was my opening line on a bus ride I still remember in singular detail all these decades later, one of that handful of scenes from a person's life that, for whatever reason, stamps itself into your memory and takes root.

Picture a dark and stormy night. A Greyhound bus barreling down two-lane blacktop through the wasteland of the Iron Range. The bus filled to capacity, the interior murky, smoke so thick you can write your name in it.

I'm crammed into a window seat somewhere in the middle, next to a tall skinny blonde. We're both smoking.

"So, um, who's your favorite Beatle?" I ask Blondo, trying to flick my ash nonchalantly.

We've been riding in silence ever since pulling out of the old hometown. I've never spoken to her before, but I know who she is. She was a year ahead of me in school, a lifetime ahead in cool. I'm heading back to the U after a weekend home, during which I slept for twenty-seven hours and ate three pies. Blondo's heading back to Hollywood for all I know.

"My favorite Beatle? John, who else," yawns Blondo, slouching further into herself. She might be seven feet tall. The overhead light shines on her golden head like a tiara. "He's so far out. Like Jesus."

What I'm thinking is,

"John?! The scary smart one?! Jesus!!"

What I say is,

"Yeah, John's neat, um, cool." I'm wondering if I should chance a trip to the bathroom to augment my makeup. Blondo's eyes are like forty-fives. The records, not the pistols.

"Right on," says Blondo, taking a long drag of her Kool, rearranging some beads. "So how about you? Who's your favorite? Wait a sec, lemme guess." She turns, studies me. "I'd say ... George. Definitely George."

"That's ... like ... am*a*zing!" I say, trying not to hiccup. "How'd you know? How could you tell?"

Blondo exhales slowly. She smiles, her turquoise eyes are shadowed pools. She leans closer.

"I did something, it changed everything," she says. "I *see* things now ... I broke on through."

"Through what?" I'm picturing some sort of B&E crime spree — her neighbor's house, Teske's Jewelry, Merchants and Miners Bank.

"To the *other side*," she says, lowering her voice. "You know, like the Doors." She looks around, as if for a better camera angle. "I dropped *acid*."

"On what?" The words are out before I can take them back. I get brain freeze remembering what a dickhead I used to be.

But Blondo's heart can fill a bus, her generosity is biblical.

"*LSD*," she whispers. "I took *LSD*. Last summer. On Howard Street."

My breathing stops. My hair starts moving around on its own. At which point Blondo opens her cotton candy mouth and says,

"I saw God."

"God who?" is what I should've said. Instead I said,

"On *Howard* Street?"

This was 1969, remember, I was a fledgling, my head was full of taconite pellets, I had no perspective. I had a *wig*, for crissakes. Eventually I'd find some perspective — thanks to a tour guide called Green Pyramid — in the wallpaper of a bathroom in a farmhouse south of The City on a Halloween full moon in the future. But that was still a few years away.

This was a bus careening across the ass end of nowhere on a stormy November night in the last gasp of the sixties — last slice of pizza, last toke of the roach, last train to Clarksville, last seat on the bus — it was all up for grabs.

So I grabbed.

I smoked and stared at our reflections in the window while Blondo spun tales beside me. How God appeared to her in the Androy Hotel sign at the Fourth of July street dance last summer. How she dropped out of junior college to sell sand candles so her boyfriend could go to Canada to escape the draft. How she was growing her hair until she saw him again, sending postcards to General Delivery, Winnipeg, so she could keep him updated on its length: 1, 1-1/2, 2. No names, just numbers.

"To be on the safe side," she says, and I say,

"But how will he know what the numbers mean?" and Blondo says,

"He dropped acid, too."

I think about this and rub a circle in the moisture on the window glass. The storm seems to be loosening up. A big white X flashes past and we bump across some railroad tracks. I want to say something. I *need* to say something. Words are lining up in my throat, whole sentences, paragraphs even, all crammed into each other trying to escape.

Blondo reaches over and draws a peace sign next to my circle. My mouth opens.

"Right on," is what comes out. It's my first time saying it in real life, not just in the mirror. It feels neat, um, cool. So I try again.

"Far out."

Blondo grins and ashes her Kool and flashes me the peace sign with two long skinny nail-bitten fingers. I grin and ash and flash right back.

Meanwhile, out in the slick wet night, a big yellow moon is playing chicken between the clouds.

* * *

One bright January Saturday in 1971 I'm headed to the Harvard Market for a pack of smokes when the phone rings in my dorm room. I spent the morning talking to plants with a couple of botanists down the hall, I have to redeploy. I adjust my face and pick up.

"What's Hennepin?" I say, and Mother says,

"Shouldn't ... isn't ... 'happenin'?" and I can tell she's in full lipstick mode.

A respected elder in the Church of Latter Day Makeup, Mother taught her three daughters to be ready for our close-up even when answering the phone, not to mention entertaining the milkman or the occasional census taker. I wouldn't dream of getting out of bed in the morning without my eyebrows, thus the Maybelline pencil on my nightstand next to the Baby Ben alarm clock and well-thumbed copy of *The Hobbit*.

Ask me what I most retained from my years as an English

major at the U, I'd say J.R.R. Tolkien and Carlos Castaneda. Turns out Shakespeare and Milton had nothing on Gandalf and all those mushrooms.

My parents were in the habit of calling a couple dozen times a week to check up on me, being they were footing the bill for this adventure in higher learning, a staggering $490 per quarter.

"But *fencing?*" Mother said when I mentioned my phy ed credit a few calls back. "My stars, what will they think of next?"

What they thought of was the Strike.

The CliffsNotes: In the beginning was the War. Then came the Tet Offensive. Martin Luther King. Robert Kennedy. The Democratic Convention. My Lai. The Moratorium. The Lottery. Cambodia.

Like an exercise in math and logic, it had a certain elegance, it all made sense. Just ask Shirley Jackson.

But things fall apart, the center cannot hold, mere anarchy is loosed upon the world. Just ask Yeats.

Then came May 1970.

During a protest over the invasion of Cambodia, four students at Kent State University were shot to death by the National Guard, and all hell broke loose. Students across the country went on strike, shutting down hundreds of campuses. *"THEY CAN'T KILL US ALL!"* read a banner at NYU, but they appeared to be trying to do just that in Southeast Asia, enough was enough. Taking our cues from our profs, we negotiated our grades, sold our books, packed up our shit, and got the fuck outta Dodge.

Something was rotten, and not just in Denmark. Just ask Shakespeare.

Did I mention I was an English major?

So I promise Mother that, yes, I'm doing my sit-ups and neck exercises, and no sooner have I hung up than the phone rings again. *Guess who?*, I say to the Cosmic Oneness, and pick up.

"You'll never guess ... " says a vaguely familiar male voice, and I never do.

Not until I've gone full metal jacket on the makeup and threads — blue eye shadow, matching clogs, poncho, bell bottoms, earrings the size of parrot swings — have one last toke, and trip down the hallway into a weekend that will careen me out of a lingering girlhood and imprint itself permanently on my narrow smalltown psyche like rainbow tie-dye on virginal white cotton.

Did I mention I was a theater minor?

I sail into the dorm lobby trailing hemp and hauteur like a wake, and when I see him standing there, my first thought is, *Man what a tan!!*

The perfect tan was the primary summer job of the girls back in my hometown. We spent all available daylight hours in our backyards, marinating in baby oil, surrounded by reflector panels, transistor radios, and alarm clocks (to tell us when to turn over), before presenting like bronzed trophies to the lust of the boys and the envy of our whiter sisters, although make no mistake, we were all white as Ivory Soap to the core.

And as I stare at the guy with the world class tan, my next thought is, *What the?!*

Because a jarhead stands in the lobby of Centennial Hall on this bright white day, and this jarhead is waiting for me. It takes a few beats, then I recognize him.

Remember that song "Little Boxes," where all the houses are made of ticky-tacky and they all look just the same? I grew up in a neighborhood like that, a sort of suburb, only nobody in our town called them that. My neighborhood was built on a former cow pasture and called Greenhaven, but the townies called it Mudhaven. Not to be confused with the neighborhood built on an old mining dump where most of the doctors lived, which they called Pill Hill.

So here's this tanned, muscled jarhead, in buzzcut and fatigues, a kid I've known since junior high. A kid from the other side of the tracks, not some lame suburb, who's shown up out of the blue at the U in the winter of '71 looking for me. Back in the day the boys from the other side of the tracks were usually cuter. Usually wilder. Usually working class. And they were usually the boys who went to the War.

It's the same everywhere, just ask Fitzgerald.

As for what happened next, ask Rod Serling.

The whole scene is surreal. Here we are, this unlikely pair, just standing there, not saying much, squinting into the sun, moving our feet around. But eventually we start talking, and then after a while we head up to my dorm room, where we spend the next thirty-six hours sprawled across my kelly green area rug in a haze of Panama Red, sandalwood incense, and Camel straights, while Neil Diamond provides soundtrack on my portable Zenith hi-fi and snow falls like popcorn past the window, like we're characters inside some enormous snowglobe.

Mostly he tells stories about the jungle, but not the real stories, I'll realize much later. He tells about the heat. The green. The mosquitoes. The rainforest. He tells about enlisting with his best friend, a kid I also knew, who'd trained as a machine-gunner and been killed by a sniper, which I'd heard through the grapevine.

I tell about the U. My classes. The City. Neil Fucking Diamond.

"This is just ... the neatest ... album!!" I say, rolling another joint on the cover of *Tap Root Manuscript*. I sound like Hayley Mills.

Meanwhile, he sounds like ... a man. *There's a man in my dorm room!!* Not some sarcastic kid with a scarred lip and eyes at half-mast who used to talk out of the side of his mouth and stare at me from a distance as I went about my little teenage life with all its *sturm und drang*.

Remember that song "Love Stinks," where you love her, she loves him, he loves somebody else, you just can't win? That was us in our school days. I guess I'd known how he felt, but I was full-throttle into my first love, hurtling headlong toward my first heartbreak, and *Oh! what a ride it was!*, I might as well have been in some parallel universe.

If he remembers how it was, he doesn't cop to it. Just watches me, like he used to, only he's calmer than I remember, quieter.

And then sometime after the third or fourth joint, somewhere between "Cracklin' Rosie" and "I Am the Lion," during the third or fourth replay, the man on the kelly green rug in my dorm room snowglobe does something extraordinary, something that has stayed with me all these years.

He stands up, reaches for my hand, pulls me to my feet. He reaches into his back pocket, takes out his billfold, pulls out a photo: a faded, folded wallet-size print of my graduation picture.

"I had this with me," he says, "in country."

I stare at the photo, at him.

"You ... where?" says Hayley Mills.

"Nam," he says. "I had this with me, in country."

It's the first time I hear that phrase. It takes a few beats, then I understand. What he's saying. He carried a photo — *of me!!* — with him. In the War.

You know that old saying, "Life can change on a dime?" It's true. Or a dime bag.

If this were a novel — or an ABC miniseries — we might've gotten together. The jarhead and the boho might've hooked up, taken a shot at it, given it the old college try.

But that would be playing to the cheap seats.

After that long surreal weekend — after we'd said goodbye, and promised to keep in touch, and he'd walked away toward the Harvard Market and turned the corner and disappeared — our paths didn't cross again for many years.

Our lives unfolded in different directions ... different settings, different casts, different scripts. But the memory of that weekend stayed with me, the idea of him stayed inside me somewhere.

Then, at our twentieth high school reunion, I saw him again.

I'm there with Mr. Right, my jogger's legs, my big blonde eighties hair, and at some point I turn around in a haze of smoke and Mitch Ryder and cheapass chardonnay, and there he is — red shirt, western boots, tan. I walk over.

"Hey," I say, Hayley Mills long gone.

"Hey, yourself," he says, "long time."

"And what a long strange trip," I say.

We trade CliffsNotes: I dropped out of the U, got married, graduated, got divorced, taught for a while, waited tables, played with a few bands, met Mr. Right, got married again, still live in The City. He headed back up to the old hometown, worked in the mines for a while, got married, had a couple kids, played in a bocce ball league, got divorced, got the fuck outta Dodge, moved to Nevada, still lives in the mountains.

"So what do you do up there in those mountains?" I say, and he says,

"Pan for gold," and I say,

"Get outta town!" and he says,

"I did."

Just then, right on cue, the band launches deafeningly into "Proud Mary." If this were a novel, it would've been "Fortunate Son."

"Think they know any Neil Diamond?" I shout, and he shouts,

"Not sure they're that cool! Wanna dance?"

And we finally do.

ROLLER SKATING ON ACID

I n a last ditch effort to outrun an advancing groundswell of
bad karma, I cashed my $26 unemployment check, packed
my grandmotherly trunk, and hightailed it up Highway 61 to
the cabin, where I proceeded to roll up my sleeves and clean
where no woman has cleaned before — certainly no man — not
since the McCarthy era. Joseph, not Eugene.

And I want to say one word to you, just one word:
microfiber!

Am I the last person in the free world to discover this
miracle shit? I am seriously considering becoming a housewife.
I mean, I need a job, and the writing is on the wall. Literally,
that's how grimed up the wall is. I mean, nobody's going to hire
some over-the-hill boho has-been from the seventies whose
fondest memories of that era involve controlled substances and
roller skates.

But let's talk *microfiber!* I'm telling you, this shit cleans
anything you can think of.

Thirty-six hours in a heatwave in a building measuring no

more than 400 square feet? It was a steambath, I tell you, I could hardly wait to get back to indoor plumbingland and weigh myself. I nuked the fuck outta the joint. I half-expected the whole thing to implode at any second, like maybe the half-century of dirtgum I was excavating from every cranny might be what was holding the walls up.

If there's a War next month and we all end up at the cabin with no dishes, there won't be an inch of space off which we cannot eat.

Let me explain.

Nonviolent non-packing pacifist leftie pantheists that we are (hold the gunfire), we'd have to use all available tableware as weaponry against any wandering desperados attempting to infiltrate one of the last bastions of unsullied U.S. soil before acquiescing to our greater determination (and a seemingly endless supply of cheapass flea market crockery) and pussy-footing it over the border into Canadia.

Why undertake (I love a word with undertones) such a herculean task in the first place? I want to say one word to you, just one word: *identity crisis!*

Newly jobless childless purposeless that I am, I'm desperate to find something — *anything!* — to fill the gaps between Free Cell, Netflix, pinot grigio, and prostrate weeping. I examined the options and decided to re-up on ... *housecleaning!* With a mother who dusted the houseplants and ironed the bed linens, I'm genetically predisposed. I sandwiched in a bit of research betwixt my other occupations, and that's when I discovered ... *microfiber!*

The keyboard all but orgasmed beneath my trembling fingers.

How could I not have known? How could I have been so clueless? Maybe having a steady stream of housekeepers doing all the dirty work since the Reagan administration might have had something to do with it? My husband long ago gave up trying to figure out what it is I do all day.

Clearly the house in town needed no help from the likes of *moi*, so I set my dusty sights on the cabin. A more accurate term for which would be the compound, given the property encompasses a collection of buildings scattered across roughly forty acres. If things went as planned, there were a half dozen other skeevy filth-ridden structures lying around up there that I could tackle.

Once I got over the initial shock to my system (it was the Pine Sol), I took to this latest endeavor like a fish to water. I drink like a fish (just add wine!), I'd discovered *microfiber!* (just add water!), it was a match made in heaven. When it came to cleaning, the old muscle memory kicked right in. It's like sex, or roller skating. Not that one is inclined to engage in either of these activities once one reaches my delicate age.

In addition to the satisfaction of a job well done — not to mention the meds I'm hoping to score as a result of grievous bodily harm brought on by furniture reassignment — I also discovered that if you breathe enough 409 of an afternoon, cosmic messages begin emanating from the wallpaper and linoleum, just like the old days. Only in this case you haven't ingested anything illegal, and the couch doesn't appear to move around the room by itself like a barge for weeks afterward.

I intend to tackle the other buildings up at the compound just as soon as I can walk again. My muscles might still have good memory, but I sure as hell don't. I forget that, these days, I can injure myself yawning, let alone single-handedly nuking the fuck outta one of the last bastions of unsullied U.S. soil, *microfiber!* or no *microfiber!*

So until I'm back in action on the cleaning circuit, I've got my books and my poetry to protect me. And my $26 unemployment check and my Free Cell and my pinot grigio. Maybe I can stay tucked up here under the armpit of Canadia for the time being, in this protective forcefield of boreal forest and Lemon Pledge, and somehow keep under the radar of this groundswell of bad karma long enough to catch my breath and come up with Plan E. Maybe it's F.

* * *

In a past life I drove my daughter to school every morning. Piano on Tuesdays. Gymnastics fifty-seven times a week. A few years later I'm driving her to court appearances. Or putting her on a bus with a roundtrip ticket to whatever town the courthouse is in. Or giving her the money and telling her to figure it out herself.

These days I just block her cell number.

In the beginning my daughter's ongoing relationship with law enforcement was confined to the town we live in, eventually a couple of neighboring states. Turns out she had bigger ambitions, her career has since taken off. She's now on a cross-country tour, making the acquaintance of a random sampling of local authorities across the lower forty-eight.

It makes me nostalgic for the good old days, for the first time we ever bumped up against the U.S. justice system. There we were, a compact mother/daughter unit, in step, together, filled with hope and belief and a smidgen of comic relief. Like, no worries, just got a wee bit off track, at least we're keeping things from going south.

Dream on. It all went south, all right. And north and east and west.

. . .

So there we are, that first time, just over the bridge in another state, not to be confused with the state my daughter is usually in, which is what landed us on this little detour in the first place. We're sitting next to one another in the courtroom, on a massive wooden bench beneath a couple of century-old chandeliers, surrounded by benchfuls of other similarly unfortunate souls, like so many lambs cows pigs turkeys heading down the chute to their bitter destiny.

We're all of us poor players here, some of us poorer than others, strutting and fretting and gnawing our cuticles raw this hour upon the stage. This stage within the granite-and-marble splendor of the hall of justice, where justice may or may not be served, but something's being served down the street at the Baby-Come-Back! Baby-Back Cafe, and it ain't tofu casserole.

Because here comes the judge, all rise. And it looks like the judge might be the Baby-Come-Back!'s best customer.

One thing my daughter and I have always been good at doing together is laughing hysterically. All the way to the shrink, or the pawn shop, or the stockade, as the case may be.

Our shared humorous bone has likely saved us from extinction as a mother/daughter unit, given the abysmal familial deadzone of recent years. Our particular sense of humor is of the hyperventilating, eye-watering, pants-wetting, call-the-paramedics-I'm-choking-on-my-own-vomit variety, and it's easily triggered by certain scenes in certain movies.

Who needs a family intervention? Just sit us down in front of a cut of John Candy flipping pancakes with a shovel in *Uncle Buck*, or Jane Fonda shooting Nyquil in the bathroom mirror in *Monster-In-Law*, next thing you know we're doubled over in each other's arms snortling uncontrollably (a snort-chortle hybrid). Or make it anywhere Melissa McCarthy shows up in *Bridesmaids*. Or when Mumble the penguin starts dancing in *Happy Feet*, for which we were politely asked to leave the theater at the Mall of America when my daughter was eight.

So my first thought was of my daughter when, during a segment of *Comedy Central* on Netflix a while back, a rather super-sized comedian cautioned the audience not to call her "fat" but "hard to kidnap." I spit a mouthful of Corona into my lap and reached for my cell phone.

My second thought was whether or not they let you watch *Comedy Central* in the stockade.

You might say the judge is hard to kidnap.

I pointed this out to my daughter that first time, as we sat on that hard hard bench in the hall of justice awaiting, well, justice, and she spit a mouthful of Smartwater into her lap. And as any madwoman knows, even more difficult than trying to control your bladder while cackling maniacally, is trying to do it soundlessly. Not to mention whilst sitting on a hard hard bench awaiting justice, whether or not justice is on the menu that particular day in that particular corner of the free world.

Want fries with that?

You might say my daughter was born into injustice. That it was there at her birth, like a caul. That it's followed her around like a shadow, a presence, a journey haunted by the luck of the draw. She's the original changeling, exchanged for something that never existed. The kidnapped child who can never go back, there is no ransom, no there there.

It's a long afternoon, in that courtroom. Case after case, the line shuffles forward. The judge sits in judgement. The chandeliers shine on. Eventually my daughter stops snortling, looks around her, starts sweating to the roots of her this-week-green-

and-magenta hair. The clock ticks. The feet shuffle. My daughter sweats.

Then, like a wake-up call, like last call, it's over. The gavel comes down. "Next!" barks the judge, and we exit the courtroom, me fighting the urge to genuflect. I leave my daughter in the Women's and head for the parking lot.

And as the locals are lining up down at the Baby-Come-Back!, I'm skulking at the curb in the getaway vehicle, congratulating myself on successfully beating the odds in rescuing someone from the long arm of the law. Which in this particular courtroom with this particular judge is not so much long as it is wide. Make that double-wide, with add-on screen porch. The scales of justice, indeed.

I remember watching my daughter leave the hall of justice building, running like all hell was after her down the wide marble steps, taking them two-at-a-time, finishing her grand exit with a perfectly executed roundoff-back-handspring series across the courtyard to the waiting car.

"I fucking stuck it!!" she gasps, landing in the seat beside me, and we high-five it.

I start my engine. I remember feeling relief, like a celebration was in order. Like a dicey situation had been navigated. Like we'd put an end to something.

Dream on. Turns out it was only a beginning.

* * *

The day after my birthday I went for a run, tripped on a rock, fell in the road, and fucked up my rotator cuff. I limped home cradling my arm like the baby I never had, blood streaming from my knee onto the putting-green grass between headstones, and it occurred to me, not for the first time, perhaps the cemetery was a poor choice of venue.

I hobbled up the front steps, collected the mail (*Birthday Greetings!* from the Social Security Administration), cracked open a Corona, and googled "fucked-up shoulder injury." I didn't know I had a rotator cuff.

Later that same day my daughter, her boyfriend, her recently-released-on-parole cat, and a suitcase of kickass weed moved in with us. I was sitting with my husband in the sun in the living room, nursing my battle scars with my third or seventh Corona, watching the daughter, the boyfriend, and the cat move all their worldly possessions up to the second floor, and my only thought was,

"There goes the neighborhood."

This was after the furnace exploded and before the sewer backed up and during the distemper epidemic, of which we were as yet unaware, despite the cross section of local wildlife, including four raccoons, three gray foxes, and a quintet of skunks, who'd been squatting under the house for the last month, much as the daughter, *et al.*, were now doing aboveground. Thus one might conclude we'd already tipped the balance of the hood in our favor, if favor is the right word.

Of course the smog of secondhand hemp hadn't yet begun billowing from our windows, the jury was still out.

What's a jobless, battle-scarred, red-blooded American has-been of a certain age to do?

I started to clean. I cleaned nonstop for the next six months, pausing only for my daily constitutionals to the cemetery and the liquor store, before crashing in the third-floor Barcalounger to binge-watch *Mob Wives*. I mean, where's Drita when ya need ha? Getting her tits retreaded, that's where, I should be so lucky.

Before that afternoon in May when she showed up on our doorstep cat in hand, our daughter hadn't lived with us in over two years. Now she was nineteen. It doesn't take a rocket scientist to do the math. Or a mental health professional. Or law enforcement. Thanks to those two years and change, our daughter now had intimate relationships with two out of the three. In several states.

This kid was born with a full set of baggage. A suitcase of pot was just carry-on.

CRASH TEST

After our daughter ran away for the third time — the charm? — the first thing we did was change the locks on all the doors. Then we locked them. She was a month shy of seventeen.

"Typical teenage stuff," people told us, "their frontal lobes don't develop until they're twenty-five, won't last, take a stress pill."

Make mine time-release morphine. People were clueless.

While the mother three doors down fretted over her typical teenager wearing too much eyeliner, our typical teenager was stealing whatever she could get her hands on from whoever crossed her path, pawning jewelry, pocketing cash, palming credit cards, taking our cars out for joyrides in the dead of night sans permit or license, shoplifting, skipping school, running away, drugging tattooing piercing cutting herself ...

... if this was typical, sign me up for the Mars Mission.

We were shaken but not surprised, having learned long ago what a gifted little thespian our daughter was. She could play the part, say the right thing, look you straight in the eye, and prevaricate like there was no tomorrow. And now there was. No tomorrow.

Now she'd ransacked the house one last time, crammed what she could into an armful of paper bags, and tore-ass out the front door down to a getaway driver waiting at the curb, and they'd shot off into the middle of a snowstorm in the middle of the night like a couple of crash test dummies, leaving me, my husband, and the dog in the middle of the living room in the middle of our disbelief, all our good intentions drifting lifeless around us.

It put the fallout into the nuclear part of family.

July Fourth. My husband and I are at the cabin, getting ready to head down to the lake — watch the moon rise, drink some wine, light some sparklers, a real blowout celebration — when the phone rings. The dog, who's been waiting patiently by the door, gives me a look. I should've listened to her.

It's the neighbor, a retired cop, back at the house in town.

"Sorry to bother you," she says, "but I was wondering, do you have people staying at your house while you're away?"

"No ... " I say.

"Well, then, I think somebody might've broken in," she says.

The dog, who can hear sounds only God can hear, heard it before I did.

You know that feeling when you're looking forward to something, something long in coming, something you think you deserve because you've been through a fucking meatgrinder, and the joke's on you because you don't even eat meat? Hold that feeling. Now, far in the distance, barely audible but growing louder by the nanosecond, you hear it: the meatgrinder. Steady, sure, unstoppable. And it's coming for you.

What does a raked over the coals, over the hill, hungover

chunk of mincemeat do? You throw the dog a Nylabone and hunt around for the corkscrew.

Turns out our daughter put a crew together and broke into the house in town, decamping with all the liquor, cash, canned goods, paper products, and lawn ornaments they could carry, before tear-assing down the alley in an escape junker just as the cop next door was crossing the lawn.

Apparently this was our daughter's way of celebrating Independence Day, a full moon and sparklers *de rigueur* in her movie.

Then my husband's best friend died.

He'd survived a stroke, a brain bleed, two weeks in ICU, and a year of painstaking recovery, then took his 12-gauge out for a walk in the woods at midnight in a snowstorm.

Then the dog died.

The cat died in the eye of the squall, when the kid was still living at home, followed by the plecostomus, who at twenty-one had seen it all from its fifty-gallon sound-proof booth, like a fifties quiz show. But the husky had held on, waiting for the calm after the storm, the smoke to clear after the battle, the quiet that descended like a shroud.

Then they fired my ass.

The new director of the school where I'd been teaching for more than a decade decided she wanted new blood, my blood was old. Suddenly I found myself home alone, resident mail-opener, newspaper-reader, coffee-maker, floor-pacer, hair-puller, nail-biter, with only the shadows and the phone for company.

Then the calls started.

After a while they blended into one another, one long running dialogue: if this was Tuesday, must be the Sheriff,

Friday, the Police, Sunday, the ER. They continued for months, like the phases of the moon, a pre-recorded *"This is the* (fill in the blank) *County Jail, will you accept a call from an incarcerated loved one?"* the default voicemail.

And through it all, whenever I drove up the alley and into the driveway and got myself out of the car and through the gate and down the sidewalk to the back door, no one was home. The house was dark, the kid was on the lam, my husband was at work, all the animals were dead. Even the ghosts were laying low.

We still had our landline — we called it the landmine — and headed for the basement whenever it rang. We expected a bomb to drop at any moment and kept the basement wine cellar — we called it the bomb shelter — well-stocked. At any given time we couldn't tell you where our daughter was, who she was with, even *if* she was, a feeling inconceivable in a normal family. Whatever that means.

And this is how we lived, in a sort of suspended animation, waiting for whatever shoe store was going to drop next.

The months piled up, and the miles.

The blue drug house with holes in the walls, people passed out in the hallway, eighteen-wheelers streaking past the front door morphed into somebody's uncle's basement, somebody's brother's back room, somebody's boyfriend's van.

A campground in Nevada morphed into a beach in Southern Cali, a tent in Humboldt County, an abandoned outbuilding in eastern Oregon, and finally, the shoulder of I-84 in Idaho, and the bus a State Trooper put our daughter on to send her back to her home state, instead of his other option, a holding cell. An option chosen by other authorities, at other times, in the not-too-distant future.

Which is how we found ourselves picking her up at the local bus terminal late one summer evening and driving home through a thunderstorm, while she sat in the back seat wolfing a BK veggie burger and regaling us with stories from the road. Had the Statie finally scared the shit out of her? was she relieved to be a civilian again? was she glad to be back in the land of seven-month winters? was she fucking hallucinating??

The only thing we knew for certain was that we hadn't heard our daughter's voice in a long time, and she was talking, nonstop, to us. Who weren't hallucinating.

We dropped her off downtown, where she'd be staying with a transgendering friend from the alternative school days, in an alley-entrance walk-up studio above a fast-food Chinese joint and a former three-two bar, window on an airshaft, bathroom down the hall, City Police Precinct half a block away.

The Garret, we called it, and it would be her home for the better part of a year, during which time she would sell enough hemp for the down payment on a car; keep up a day job for appearances; dye her waist-length hair a different color every week; cut all her hair off and start over; keep the tattoo artists on First Street in business; stay out of jail; earn her high school diploma.

My husband and I got down on our knees (what was left of them) and thanked the cosmos at large for the diploma (I called the adult learning center to confirm), then summoned the extended pack (what was left of it) for a grad party — watch the moon rise, drink some wine, light some sparklers, a real blowout celebration.

Two months later our tattooed daughter with the short short hair, her boyfriend, her recently released-on-parole cat, and a suitcase of kickass weed moved in with us. They stayed for six months. During which time nobody died, nobody went to jail, nobody gave birth, nobody was abducted by aliens, and the house was spotless.

The charm.

It lasted just shy of a year.

* * *

Once there was a family.

They lived in the far north of north in a three-bedroom rambler in an old mining town on the wilds of the Mesabi Iron Range. The father was a salesman and smoked a cigar and wore a suit and tie and drove a company car. The mother was a housewife and smoked Tareytons and wore a housedress and lipstick and drove a Kirby upright. The daughters were Baby Boomers and wore their parents out and drove them crazy.

The other men on the block were miners and wore coveralls and drove Euclids and made fun of this father for his failure to beget boys. This father found himself in this godforsaken outpost because of his daughters' blue-eyed black-haired mother, and he tried to rise above it all — with his La Palinas, his piano, his great abiding brain, and his great abiding love for the wild, which surrounded them on all sides.

Also surrounding them on all sides was a secret. And back in the fifties, which is where this story begins, secrets were kept well hidden — in the backs of closets, under the wall-to-wall carpeting, behind the piano. But it's difficult to keep hiding an elephant behind a piano no matter how talented the piano player.

Once there was a family. Jazzman father, northern belle mother, and sisters three — firstborn, middle, and little sister, the elephant. All cellophaned up in their Donna Reed delusion of a postwar American family. It doesn't take a rocket scientist to do the math.

. . .

When little sister had her first convulsion, middle sister was three, likely entertaining some imaginary friend in some out of the way corner:

"Nice to see you, Madame Schumann-Heink! Have a zweiback! Have some tea!"

Meanwhile, out in the hallway, her one-year-old sibling has taken a header onto the floorboards and is trying to swallow her tongue.

The jazzman found himself routinely saving his youngest child's life — he'd worked as a lifeguard when he was a teenager and learned resuscitation — while the rest of the family stood by in horror and watched. The doctors piled up, the trips downstate, the diagnoses, the medications. But nothing helped.

The seizures continued for two years, until, out of the blue, they stopped.

Just like that.

Was it the local MD the parents had finally gone to in a last desperate effort? Who'd asked all the questions, examined the toddler, showed the parents how to stretch her anus to help with bowel movements, and told them to keep this up until the issue resolved itself.

Which it did. The family was stunned. It was a miracle. The nightmare was over. But the damage was done.

Coke-bottle glasses, correctional shoes, slow on the uptake, last in line. Little sister was the kid you made fun of, didn't want to hold hands with, didn't want to sit next to. Middle sister has a lasting memory of little sister clinging to their mother's housedress like a barnacle — or a Siamese twin, like the ones middle sister had sneaked a peek at in *Life* — while their mother went about her day vacuuming, dusting, cooking, ironing. Other kids routinely followed little sister home from school, kicking her lunchbox, knocking her down, throwing anything they could get their hands on at her, and once, poking her with hat pins.

If middle sister happened to be around, she'd go after these little mouthbreathers like a demon from hell. But she was busy with her own life, adding to her CV with more extracurriculars than you could shake a baton at. She wanted to be, at one time or another: a detective, a dancer on Broadway, a skater in Ice Capades, a skater in Roller Derby, a famous pianist, a famous actress, a famous author, famous. She also wanted to be a good sister, but often failed, and dealt with her failure by pushing on her eyeballs until the colored lights appeared; chewing her nails down to the quick; reciting the alphabet backwards while dodging sidewalk cracks; or just giving in to it all and smacking her head with a hairbrush.

No one in the family talked about any of this. Denial clung to them like ore dust. The northern belle's rose-colored glasses were firmly in place, while the jazzman, like most fifties fathers, was generally absent from his daughters' lives, except when it came to things like spankings, piano lessons, heading to the woods for a Christmas tree, or escorting them to the Shrine Circus or the County Fair or the above-mentioned local MD for booster shots.

At one point, for reasons known only to her, the northern belle started dressing her two younger daughters alike — identical outfits, identical pixie haircuts — and middle sister started thinking they were twins. Regular, not Siamese. Middle sister was six or seven, she'd been entertaining invisible friends since her crib days, in her world anything was possible. But the jig was up the summer she was ten, when the whole family crammed into the Chevy station wagon with the owl face on the rear end and drove out to visit relatives in New Jersey.

While getting ready for a much-anticipated day trip to

New York City, the northern belle accidentally stuffed middle sister into little sister's identical butterscotch sundress, and off they all went. Radio City Music Hall, Times Square, Empire State Building, Statue of Liberty — four adults and seven kids tripped the light fantastic (little sister was back in Jersey with the babysitter), until the northern belle happened to glance out the window of the tour bus as it pulled away from the curb in Chinatown. There was her middle daughter strolling happily along the crowded sidewalk, sucking on a candy cigarette and waving a delicate souvenir fan, all decked out in her favorite red patent leather T-straps and a way-way-way-too-small dress.

The firstborn came to middle sister's rescue. Which was surprising, given they'd been mortal enemies ever since the firstborn had offered to rock the new baby in its cradle and accidentally tipped it onto the floor. Which was before the time she'd offered to push it around the apartment in its stroller and accidentally rolled it down the backstairs. But who's counting?

The Chinatown Incident was the beginning of a beautiful friendship.

"She looks like a complete buttonhead," said the firstborn, co-opting one of their father's favorite insults. "Pull-ease, Mother, get her some different clothes ... a twist blouse? a kilt? Kickerinos?"

Possibly the firstborn considered her sister's lack of curb-appeal a threat to her burgeoning social life — she collected boyfriends like charms on a bracelet and was always running for queen of one thing or another — only middle sister couldn't care less. She'd finally broken free from something.

Little sister didn't break free until high school, when she showed up for tenth grade like the new kid in school. Long Summer Blonde hair, buckets of makeup, way-way-way-too-short skirts — over the summer little sister had morphed from bully-magnet into Sixties It Girl, ala Edie Sedgwick or Twiggy.

Gone were the Coke-bottle glasses, the correctional shoes. So what if she was slow on the uptake? if her ankles turned in? if the world was a bit fuzzy?

Suddenly there was a new game in town, and this new game was accessible to this new girl, something she instinctively understood. Little sister had discovered sex, and she never looked back.

Fast forward a few years.

Little sister finds herself, at twenty-two, at a military base in the South Pacific, married to a handsome jarhead husband and surrounded by a cadre of stray cats, insects the size of hubcaps, monsoons the size of small countries, and a colicky screaming baby. One day she packs up the baby, staggers to the car, drives through a monsoon to the base hospital, and demands they take it back. Pleads, cajoles, threatens, and finally faints. But the military has a strict no-returns policy.

What's a red-blooded American military spouse of questionable mental health hanging on by a thread on the other side of the planet to do? Fly home to the motherland and get a divorce, dragging the baby behind her. Who continues to scream, on and off, for years and years.

When middle sister first meets her, the baby is teetering around in her grandparents' living room wearing a diaper, a tiara and a rabbit fur stole, and middle sister falls in love. Just like that. This is several years before middle sister's *aha!* moment concerning fur, not to mention babies, and several years after she's worn the outfit herself, *sans* diaper, at her high school prom.

It's also the beginning of a new chapter in her long loss of innocence regarding love. Which isn't enough.

Little sister stays at the family home just long enough to

shed the baby weight, if not the baby, before cutting her losses and hitting the road, baby on board.

Little sister's loveliness, her easiness, her chameleonic charm draws people to her, men mostly, but there's trouble in River City, and she spirals from job to job, man to man, crisis to crisis. She learns her way around a stripper pole and the backseat of a taxi, which low-rents are child-friendly, where to go for abortions, and with help from her ADC check, manages to keep cobbling the money together.

Meanwhile, the baby screams and stutters and wets the bed and pulls out her hair by the handfuls and spends much of her life by herself, while her mother goes about making a living, if not a life.

Then one dark and stormy night some biker little sister has been fucking blows a hole in the ceiling of the latest low-rent with a shotgun, and the shit hits the fan along with the plaster. It's a sound heard round the family tree, but too late. The elephant has long since left the barn.

So little sister takes the advice of some other biker mamas and hits the road again, this time for Where Else, California, a popular destination in the seventies. The firstborn has been living there for several years and has nothing but wonderful things to say. Which is pretty much all she has to say about anything, having been in SoCal long enough for it to take. Now two of the sisters are lost in La La Land, one in tarot cards and past lives, the other in lap dances and taxis.

Meanwhile, the baby grows up. Stops stuttering, stops pulling her hair out, starts looking around. Punk tomboy with purple mohawk? high school dropout? foxy white supremacist? The years tick by, the baby keeps searching. Goth party-girl? cokehead cosmetologist? wannabe gangbanger? The baby tries them all, and then some. And then something takes. And then it takes over. And then it takes everything.

. . .

When the baby discovered meth, that's all she wrote. A neverending story with only one ending.

And as if to balance the scales of all those possible babies her mother had failed to give life to, and all that possible life her mother had failed to give her, she embarks on a decades-long joyride, blowing out the lights of her world one by one, while giving birth to five living babies of her own, before leaving them, one by one, for someone else to raise.

The firstborn, a girl, she leaves on her aunt's doorstep. And the girl on the doorstep becomes middle sister's daughter. Because of love.

Which isn't enough.

WILDLIFE REHAB

My husband is the first to see her.

Dusk, late spring, we're locking doors, turning on lights, when he stops and stares into the backyard.

"There's something ... out there ... under the pergola ... " he says.

"The parabola? the parallelogram? the pentagon?" I refuse to use a word like pergola.

"A dog ..." he says.

It's been over a year, but my heart lurches.

"No ... a fox!" says my husband. "A fucking fox!"

We live in a place where he might've said fucking deer, fucking moose, fucking bear — or up at the cabin, fucking wolf, fucking cougar — all of which we've encountered at one time or another, only not in the backyard of the house in town, which is surrounded on all sides by a twenty-foot privacy fence.

I glance through the patio door, and sure enough, a fox is standing out under the polygon, silhouetted in the fading light.

Over the following weeks the fox becomes a part of our lives. She's a gray, or silver fox, and appears regularly at dusk, pausing to get her bearings before trotting across the grass and disappearing under the fence on her nightly hunt.

Before long we're hearing intermittent thumps beneath the bump out room at the back of the house, and two young kits begin appearing in the yard close to the house, blinking and looking around them in the spring air.

According to the local wildlife rehab center, this is a vulnerable time for the little family, best not to move them if possible. But, they assure us, all three will vacate once the kits are old enough, the last place a fox wants to live is in close proximity to humans. I'll drink to that.

Being canine, they're filling a void in our hearts, and we settle in for the duration and keep the cameras rolling. Little do we know this is only the tip of the iceberg. Make that the bunker.

One evening I walk out the back door to find four shadowy forms sitting around on the deck furniture, like one of those prints of dogs playing poker. It's a mother raccoon and three babies, who appear to be living under the house on the side opposite the foxes. Then a crew of skunks starts showing up in the vicinity of the birdfeeder, and it finally dawns on us: we're running a bed-and-breakfast for single-parent families from the local wildlife demographic.

Without a dog as resident bouncer, word's getting out, our occupancy rate is soaring. What's a couple of bunny-hugging-boomer-wino-veg-heads to do? Open another bottle and start naming names.

"Hon, is that Kev or Steve over by the birdbath?"

"I think it's Persephone ... her mom's at the store, they're handing out coupons for fresh roadkill."

"Shouldn't that be 'pawing out', hon?"

"Ha ha ha! Oh look, Jill finally made it up onto the swing! Next she'll be wanting a bike!"

"Oh, hon, it doesn't get much better than this ... or this Malbec, either, hon ... please, may I have some more?"

But all of us, human and fur-bearer alike, are living in a fool's paradise. Which, looking back on it, would've been a good name for our little underground railroad operation.

I never gave it a second thought when I brought one of the dogs in for their rabies or distemper shots. I knew about rabies since childhood, because that's how Old Yeller died, the first experience of the death of a beloved pet for many of my generation. But I didn't know much about distemper.

The first sign that something was wrong came when I began seeing the fox at midday.

I'd glance out the window, she'd be sitting in the yard, ears twitching, head shifting. Fifteen or twenty minutes later she'd still be there. Anthropomorphizer that I am, I decided that she felt safe in our townie fortress and was taking a few moments to relax before resuming her busy life. Somewhere in the back of my mind the thought persisted that foxes are nocturnal, but it took the skunks to bring it to the fore.

Foxes and raccoons are one thing, skunks quite another. Not that they aren't endearing. Sweet-faced, innocent, not a menacing hair on their little striped heads. But they're skunks, with a singular line of defense capable of rendering even the most fearless of species helpless and begging for mercy. Both of our dogs had been skunked — both huskies, tough and cool and self-actualized — and it only took once. Nobody fucks with skunks. Certainly not twice. And now we had ourselves a yardful.

My husband, the Skunk Whisperer, has on several occasions managed to live-trap a skunk and transport him or her into the witness protection program over in the next county, and each time he's come out smelling like a rose. Sort of. But this time there were too many, he said, enough is enough.

Which is how we came to make the acquaintance of our friendly neighborhood wildlife relocator. We didn't know we had one.

Stone Creek was the name on his card, and he showed up loaded for bear. One of the few animals he hasn't yet been able to live trap and relocate, he told us. Although he can send a bear packing most of the time with a blast from his trumpet, which he keeps stored in the back of his van alongside stacks of live traps, cases of canned tuna, and bags of Cheerios and sawdust.

We were standing with Stone in the backyard when a raven screamed. And I know a raven when I hear one, they don't call me the Raven Whisperer for nothing. Turns out it was a sound app on Stone's phone, and it was the beginning of a beautiful friendship. But it was the end of our happy little backyard Eden. Up until Stone Creek, we knew nothing about the distemper epidemic that was raging all around us.

"It's very localized," he told us, "just this area. Kills skunks, raccoons, gray fox. I've never seen anything like it, just sweeps through, kills 'em all."

I stared at him. The raven screamed again. He let it go to voicemail.

"But they've been living under the bump out since spring," I said. "Maybe it's kept them safe? I mean, how do they get ... distemper?"

"Contact with another animal who's got it," he said. "Their urine, or scat. It's highly contagious. Extremely."

I was thinking about the fox heading off into the dark every night.

"Believe me, you'll know if they have it," Stone said. "Takes a week or two for the smaller animals, a month, maybe six weeks for the fox. They slow down, barely move, get this far-away look."

Like they're stoned, I was thinking. Like up a creek.

"Just keep an eye on 'em, and let me know, " he said, and started setting up his live traps.

In forty-eight hours Stone Creek, Wildlife Relocator live-trapped five skunks and four raccoons in our backyard Eden in town. He made the requisite trips to the rehab center, where each animal was pronounced healthy and vaccinated, then he relocated them miles out in the woods, far from the killing zone. On his last trip he brought the raccoons by the house so I could say good-bye, three shadow babies hiding behind shadow Mom, four pairs of masked eyes blinking at me from a cage in the recesses of his van.

Skunks and raccoons are easy, Stone said, not so foxes. Foxes are smart, careful, distrustful. He hadn't yet been able to live trap a healthy fox, not even with tuna.

But we believed, my husband and I, we were hopeful. We rooted for the little fox family as if they were our own, three little canines in our keeping. It was impossible not to. And it consumed our lives for one long desperate week.

I'd text my husband at work:

"Clover is under the birdfeeder!"

"Allen is taking a siesta in the sun on the deck!"

"Mom just snuck under the fence to go for takeout!"

And all the while, that word: *nocturnal*. Fox are nocturnal. All our sightings were occurring in the bright light of day.

Then one morning I text my husband that Mom's enjoying a coffee break under the birdbath, and I step out onto the deck to check up on her. I clear my throat. She doesn't move, doesn't flick an ear. This is an animal who used to vanish in a heartbeat if she so much as saw my shadow in a window. I clear my throat again. I rattle a deck chair. I call Stone.

In the end, none of them made it.

One by one, over the course of a week, they were gone. One by one Stone lifted them from where they lay, unknowing in the grass, and placed them carefully in a carrier, then transported them to the wildlife center, where they were euthanized.

It was all too close to home, all too familiar. We were blindsided, overwhelmed.

And in the end, I couldn't help but envision a story·

The fox had chosen to make her den where she did because it felt safe, somehow, because it was off the beaten track, because it was far removed from ... something ... out there. The fox had known, somehow. She'd been smart. She'd found a place to hide.

And in the end, she did find it. The perfect place. In our hearts.

STRAW HOUSES

When my husband burned down the garage, I could've said,

"This is the last straw."

Except according to my husband, I'm as much to blame as the next guy, the next guy being my husband. So I said,

"Those who live in straw houses shouldn't smoke," or something like that, and went in search of a buddha.

This was no desperate eleventh hour purchase. I spent hours in the cloud, in a fog of pinot grigio and nag champa, navigating countless websites for just the right vibe, just the right energy, until a singular piece of statuary spoke to me.

"Any port in a storm of bad karma," it said, and I punched Proceed to Checkout.

I suppose one shouldn't use words like "punched" when discussing buddhas, so let's say "selected." I selected a buddha from out of the cosmic vastness, trusting it was just the buddha for me, and held my breath as it made its way along the FedEx astral plane from the wilds of (where else) California to my smoky doorstep.

When my buddha finally arrived, I lugged the heavy parcel over the sill into the mudroom, carefully cut away the infinite layers of swaddling, and beheld my iconic new friend for the first time. Who had no head.

Luckily this was noon. I was already coffeed to the ovaries, my brain was open for business. But I checked again, store policy. It was true. My buddha had pulled a Marie Antoinette somewhere out on I-90.

I don't know, is it just me? Or would the next guy consider it a bad sign if a buddha showed up headless on her doorstep?

At first I thought I'd misread the description, maybe this was one of those Some Assembly Required buddhas. But then I discovered the head down by the buddha's knee, with no hope of reconciliation, and the writing was on the wall:

"The storm rages on," it said, "batten down the hatches."

Maybe it should've said,

"Quit while you're a head."

The morning the garage burned down, I woke up. So far, so good. I lurched out of bed, staggered to the window, yanked open the curtain, and squinted into the sunshot light.

My first thought was that there'd been an ebola outbreak in the alley. A squad of what appeared to be humans in full body protection was moving around down there, awkwardly but determinedly, and it took my brain a few seconds to process what I was seeing. Who am I kidding. It took fifteen minutes.

Then finally, enlightenment:

Firefighters! Fighting a fire! Hoses! Explosions! Smoke! Neighbors! The whole ball of wax!

Another ten minutes, another lightbulb moment:

The!! Garage!! Is!! Burning!! The!! Fuck!! Down!!

Eventually I managed to get myself assembled and out into

the backyard, where I was duly apprised of the whole gruesome turn of events by a bevy of onlookers.

As the story goes, one of the neighbors, out for a walk with her dog, noticed smoke streaming from our garage and called 911 on her cell, then hot-footed it over to our bunker and commenced banging on the patio door. History has it that Nero fiddled while Rome burned, and that's how the neighbor found my husband: fiddling with the kitten while the garage went up in flames.

Earlier that morning, during a momentary psychotic break, my husband had emptied what he believed to be dead ashes into the garbage can in the garage, operative words in that sentence being "psychotic" and "dead." The ashes were from a small fire we'd had the previous evening in our portable fire pit on the patio, which is where I come in. Not in the fire pit, in the story.

"It's your fault," said my husband, "for two reasons."

This was hours after the fire. After the firefighters and the neighbors — and the neighbors' kids and the neighbors' dogs and the neighbors' manservants and the neighbors' maidservants and the neighbors' cattle — were gone. After the shock and chagrin over what had happened had made a permanent home in our already shocked and chagrined psyches. After the coffee, and before the cocktails, in that between place where most of life gets lived, not with a bang (of paint cans exploding) but a whimper.

"Have you lost your mind?" I said to my husband.

We were back in the house by now, playing with the kitten, loathe to ever step foot in our backyard again, where the blackened wraith of the ghost of garages past loomed ever menacing and pungent just beyond the privacy fence. Which miraculously had remained intact, though privacy had gone up in smoke along with everything else, given the hole in the fabric of the universe where the section of privacy that was once garage used to be.

I'd already come up with the buddha plan, and had a dozen websites queued, ready for perusal.

"I'm ordering a full body burka, too," I said, tossing the kitten a ball the size of her head. No chance of *that* making it down her little gullet. "I never want to show my face in this sooty neighborhood again."

"Don't change the subject," said my husband.

"And the subject sure as shit isn't roses, everything stinks." I squinted at him. "And none of this is my fault," I said, whether or not it was true.

"Wrong," said my husband. "If you'd just stayed by the fire last night, instead of luring me inside to ... you know ... I would've been thinking clearly this morning, I wouldn't have pulled such a bonehead move."

"Oh, I get it," I said, "it's the old chicken/egg thing ... which came first, the boner or the bonehead?" And I said it again, "Have you lost your mind?"

"And secondly," said my husband, ignoring me, moving right along in his presentation, "if you hadn't been sleeping one off, as usual, and had been drinking coffee with me on the deck this morning, you would've seen my mistake and would've stopped me from emptying those ashes into that fucking plastic can."

"I think that's an oxymoron," I said, as the kitten suddenly went berserk.

"*I'm* an oxy moron," said my husband, "and *you* should've stopped me."

This is where I could've said, for the third time,

"*Have you lost your fucking mind?!?*"

And given that less than a month later, a certain buddha

would show up, let's say "compromised" on our doorstep, this would've been a rather prophetic thing to say.

But I was thinking of my husband, of his great temple of a heart, now so full of shame and oxymorosis. And on my way to the wine bottle, I stopped and hugged him for a few seconds. Or maybe it was fifteen minutes.

"I believe it might be cocktail hour in Tibet ... " is what I said, whether or not it was true.

ABOUT THE AUTHOR

Carolyn Colburn received an MFA in Writing from Goddard College and has been awarded a Loft-McKnight Fellowship and a Minnesota State Arts Board Grant. She has worked as a musician, teacher, typesetter, and contract writer. *Minimum Maintenance*, a novel, was published in 2010. Ms. Colburn divides her time between a 100-year-old house in Duluth and a cabin on Lake Superior near the Canadian border.

Learn more at www.runningwildpress.com

Running Wild Press publishes stories that cross genres with great stories and writing. RIZE publishes great genre stories written by people of color and by authors who identify with other marginalized groups. Our team consists of:

Lisa Diane Kastner, Founder and Executive Editor
Mona Bethke, Acquisitions Editor, Editor, RIZE
Benjamin White, Acquisitions Editor, Editor, Running Wild Press
Peter A. Wright, Acquisitions Editor, Editor, Running Wild Press
Rebecca Dimyan, Editor
Andrew DiPrinzio, Editor
Cecilia Kennedy, Editor
Barbara Lockwood, Editor
Cody Sisco, Editor
Chih Wang, Editor
Pulp Art Studios, Cover Design
Standout Books, Interior Design
Polgarus Studios, Interior Design
Nicole Tiskus, Production Manager
Alex Riklin, Production Manager
Alexis August, Production Manager

Learn more about us and our stories at www.runningwild-press.com

Loved these stories and want more? Follow us at www.runningwildpress.com, www.facebook.com/running-wildpress, on Twitter @lisadkastner @RunWildBooks @RwpRIZE